NOTHING TO NASDAQ

Secrets of leading your company to Nasdaq in four years

Giri Devanur

ISBN: 198184841X
ISBN 13: 9781981848416

Library of Congress Control Number: 2017919556
CreateSpace Independent Publishing Platform, North
Charleston, SC

Contents

Acknowledgement

Going from *Nothing to Nasdaq* is a journey of lifetime even though we took Ameri100 to Nasdaq in under four years. I wanted the story to capture the highs and lows of entrepreneurial journey as well as provide a framework for other entrepreneurs and executives to lead their companies to the highest levels of corporate life.

For many years, I didn't tell anyone that I was thinking of writing a book. A bunch of my colleagues kept asking me to document some of the successes, failures and wild roller coaster journeys.

I want to thank my brother & founder of Ameri100 Dev Srinidhi for helping me lead the company to Nasdaq. He worked relentlessly for all those 4 years and helped the company reach its potential.

I also want to thank Archana, my loving wife who has managed my professional ride. I also want to thank my children Ashay and Ananya for being very supportive of my journey to achieve my goals.

I want to thank Ameri100 board members Jeff Eberwein, Dru Rai, Bob Pearse, Bala KV and Dimitrios who guided me through this journey.

I want to specially thank Dr. Art Langer who kept pushing me to develop a right framework which I present in this book as SNSNFTP. I am always in awe of his spirit for life!

A special thanks to Bill McDermott who has been a steadfast supporter and guide in this journey. Same goes to Nandan Nilekani and Rudy Karsan for their interviews to this book which makes it very special.

I want to thank Tom Blinten, Adam Finerman, Jason Cabico, Mike Fenton, Hannah Bible, Zander Rosenbluth, P K Ram, Saji Mathew, Hiremath, Bruce Poignant, Andy Hall, Peter Bennet and Jeff Peterson. Also I want to thank James Yee and Paul Ho-Sing-Loy for their help over last 23 years. I also cannot forget to thank Siddhartha VG (Founder of Café Coffee Day), Ravi Narayanan and Sri Somayaji.

I also want to thank my colleagues Ringo, Carlos, Brunda, Sandesh, Siri, Swati, Brent, Viraj, Manju, Leena, Ankush,

Swaroop, Krishnaswamy, Anala, Raghu who have been integral in our journey of Nasdaq.

I want to thank all investors, advisors, friends & family who helped directly or indirectly in this great journey of Nothing to Nasdaq.

I want to thank Girish & Vishnu for a great cover and team Ittisa for helping in the digital engagement of this book. I also want to thank Leena for proof-reading the entire manuscript. Additional thanks go to editors of CreateSpace in editing the manuscript. All these people read the evolving manuscript and offered advice. And because of their help, I am content with the final result.

Chapter 1
It All Starts with Nothing

Background

It all started with nothing. Literally. Every good story starts with a zero. I started with a big zero.

I came from a small town called Chikmagalur in India. Chikmagalur is about 250 kilometers from Bangalore and has a population of less than one hundred thousand. Yes, from an Indian standard, that's really a small town compared to cities like Delhi and Mumbai, which are racing toward twenty million.

I was born into a family of teachers, where education was always given the highest priority. My parents were obviously not rich, as teachers used to get paid much less when we were growing up. I recall my father's salary was five thousand rupees (approximately ninety dollars in today's dollars). My father used to ride an old bicycle all around, going from one house to another to tutor the "rich kids." This used to add to the low monthly income.

My father was a proud scholar. He had studied multiple great books, and we always had interesting guests at home discussing worldly matters. These conversations that I spent hours and days overhearing as a young boy went on to shape my entire perspective and view of the world.

Being the youngest in my family, I always looked to my brothers to lead a path for me. They inspired me to pursue computer engineering, which led me to a small engineering college that required minimal fees. I made it through college with almost nothing in hand.

In the early years of my college career, I would see seniors leave for higher studies in the United States, leaving me longing to go as well. However, knowing that my family couldn't afford such expenses, I had to pave my own path to the United States.

To accomplish that, I learned from one of my close friends, a senior from college, that I needed to learn a platform called IBM-AS/400, which was a hot skill at the time. From his guidance, I landed my first job and learned the programming in that platform. After a few months, a great opportunity arrived. I took a job with a start-up that wanted to send its first two hires to the United States. I was the second one. It felt like a dream come true.

City of Dreams—Los Angeles

I landed in Los Angeles in 1991 with only sixty dollars in hand, high hopes for the future, and absolutely no knowledge of the amazing journey that would start on that very day.

I got a really lucky break in my first assignment in the United States to work with probably one of the best salespeople I have ever known: Alan Dabbiere, the founder of Manhattan Associates. The amount of knowledge I received in my first year of working for him was out of this world.

I observed, copied, and practiced everything that Alan used to do. I almost worked two shifts: a morning shift to copy his style, substance, context, and delivery, and a late-evening shift to work on the programming!

I learned so much on my first trip to the United States; it was really fascinating. I was amazed by the entrepreneurship in America, the zeal and drive of its people, the depth and breadth of capital markets, and the ability of society to accept failures and celebration of success. Coming from India with nothing in hand, learning everything I did in LA was truly a blessing.

European Escapades

After I went back to India from the United States, I decided to go to Europe. I began to look for opportunities and potential assignments there. I visited Germany some twelve times in a year. I kept traveling all over Europe, learning multiple economies, marketing styles, people, work cultures, and so on.

I also used the weekends to travel and network with people. It was probably the freest time of my life. Again, I used zero dollars of my own money. I used all earning in those local markets to explore these beautiful countries.

Drive to San Francisco

By mid-1994, I wanted to head back to the United States. There was a contract programmer role in Topeka, Kansas, which I accepted. I started playing around with some different technologies and got exposed to an early mosaic browser written by Marc Andreessen, who was still studying in Chicago.

During those days, I developed a passion for trading in stocks. I started reading everything about stock markets. I was hoping to get into trading someday.

One day, a recruiter friend of mine called me saying that there was a contract position available in a stock brokerage in San Francisco. The only hitch was that it was a one-month contract. I had a one-year contract in Kansas.

I thought about it for a few hours and decided to take a chance. I gave my consent to the recruiter friend and took an interview. Things moved quickly, and the client wanted to start the very next Monday.

Since we didn't have enough money to buy last-minute flight tickets, my wife and I decided to drive! We packed the few things we had, got in a car, and drove eighteen hundred miles in two days. This long car ride and the events following it ended up being a pivotal time in my life.

Program to Nasdaq

In my first weeks at Montgomery Securities, not only was my contract extended, but I was also asked to work on a new project. I was asked to write a program to connect to Nasdaq, fetch some data, and create a report.

I was curious to know more about Nasdaq. I bought some magazines and books to learn as much as I could about it. I met some young trading associates in Montgomery after market hours to learn about Nasdaq. I kept learning more and more, and eventually I was deeply fascinated by Nasdaq and capital markets in general.

With zero investment, I started a new company, Ivega Technologies, in early 1997, a technology-services company focused on financial markets. I grew it from one person to one thousand people in the next eight years. In Ivega, we raised multiple rounds of venture capital and built everything organically. We exited that business successfully in 2005.

Billion-Dollar City

After a year of unexpected sabbatical for very personal reasons, one fine morning, my next idea for a venture arrived. I stumbled on one piece of information that one of the big projects in India was being shelved.

Serendipity has its ways. A quick series of turns in early 2006 led me to meet the CEO of the world's largest research park. Also, at the same time, a new chief minister of my state was keen to give a license to do a megaproject.

In a massive hurry, I assembled a team of experts, advisors, partners, potential clients, and government-policy experts and put together a mammoth three-hundred-plus-page project report. It quickly dawned on us that it was a massive undertaking. When we completed the detailed project plan, the project size had swelled to $1.2 billion, and the land required was one thousand acres.

By raising a seed round of capital, we got to work. The next year, we worked very hard to get the necessary permits and regulatory approvals to set up what was billed as India's first private research park. It generated quite a bit of media hype. It also led to vigorous scrutiny, as it involved one thousand acres of land. Opposition parties labeled the project as a "land grab."

Genius Branding?

We were wondering what the name of the project should be. One of my trusted advisors and a great teacher gave me a simple recommendation. If you are embarking on such a large project, name it in such a way that an American president (in those days it was George W. Bush) and a simple farmer in a village near our project should recognize it.

The only name we could come up with was Gandhi, but we didn't want to be confused with many other projects that bore Gandhi's name. So, in a splash of creativity, we called it GandhiCity Research Park.

GandhiCity was a name even George W. Bush and Rajaiah from Ramanagar could easily recognize and relate to.

Perfect Storm

Three things went wrong almost together. It was a perfect storm.

The first one was that India went through a chaotic uprising in late 2007 to early 2008 regarding land acquisition rights of the government. Farmers across India were literally up in arms against all state governments to protest a federal government policy called Special Economic Zone (SEZ). Our project had an SEZ approval. Riots in some states were so fierce that all politicians were scared to move ahead with SEZ policy. SEZ had become a dirty three-letter word.

The second part of the perfect storm was a political drama that unfolded in my state. There were serious tussles going on between political leaders across the spectrum. Our project was becoming collateral damage.

The third and final catalyst for the storm was the global financial meltdown. During early 2008, I had gone on a global roadshow pitching this project. I had pitched to thirty-eight global investors. Some of the most marquee names were on that list. Finally, we zeroed in on an investor who was very keen to give us the money at very attractive terms. We negotiated a term sheet of $300 million in equity and $900 million in debt.

In the next few months, this investor spent half a million dollars on various aspects of due diligence, such as the founding team, financial, legal, and political. After a few months, post due diligence, lawyers from both sides had agreed to a share purchase agreement, and we were super excited.

We were weeks away. I was getting jittery. One early morning, I got a call from a colleague that I should see the *Economic Times* (India's top financial daily). I went out and picked up a copy to see that the $1.2 billion deal had been published!

That put enormous pressure on the company as politicians, bureaucrats, and long-lost friends and family started calling with congratulations. Money brings more relatives than anything else.

The next few weeks were even more tension filled. We were expecting to close the documentation and get the money.

I flew to New York to meet the investor. After a good conversation, I realized there was something wrong in his voice.

Then came the shocker. On September 15, 2008, they filed bankruptcy.

The investor was Lehman Brothers.

In a perfect storm, even a 158-year-old financial giant can collapse.

GandhiCity became collateral damage. We tried hard to somehow save the company. But global markets had turned sour. There was simply no way of saving this project.

Midlife Crisis

They say people do one of three things in a midlife crisis. A. Get a new, fancy, expensive convertible car. B. Get a new trophy wife or girlfriend. C. Go back to college to study.

I am not a big fan of fancy cars. I didn't want anything to do with option B either, as I have been blessed with a great wife who is my best friend as well. So, the choice was obvious.

I moved back from India to the United States. I had a bucket list item: to study in an Ivy League school.

I applied to Columbia University for an MS in technology management. This was an executive-level program; hence I was expecting an easy admission.

Nothing ever comes easy.

I got a rejection! The reason was that I had been a CEO for too long, and this program was for aspiring CIOs. Hence, I was a misfit.

I was puzzled. Even though I was happy to know that I was overqualified for an Ivy League school, I really wanted to study.

I met the program director, Dr. Art Langer, and had a lengthy conversation. I was able to convince him and the rest of the committee that I was a serious student. Finally, they gave in.

The next twenty months was a grueling time. I was back in school. Being a CEO of a start-up, a husband, a father, and a student was very hard. It was also funny that I had to sit and do homework with my son, who was in high school then. My kids were having fun seeing Dad being busy with homework. My wife and kids were very supportive, and I could successfully complete my master's.

One of the students told Dr. Langer that the workload was heavy and he was not finding time to sleep. Dr. Langer, in his satiric best, quipped, "You get a lot of time to sleep when you're dead."

Dr. Langer is probably the highest-energy person I have met.

Twenty months later, after countless hours of homework, papers, and exams and a series of sleepless nights, I completed my MS degree at forty-three.

One more bucket-list item completed.

Product Start-Up

While I was studying at Columbia, I started working on a product idea. This product was about how to hire the right salespeople. Hiring a wrong salesperson on average costs a US company approximately $1.2 million, which includes salary, training, hiring, firing, and lost revenue and profit opportunities. I had made multiple sales hiring mistakes in the past. So, I thought it may be a cool idea to come up with a technology solution to avoid such bad hiring.

We called this product company WinHire and started working on building the product. It had some cool features, such as micro expression analysis to analyze the face for telling the truth. We also partnered with an Israeli start-up to analyze the voice for truth.

After months of hard work, we went on a customer discovery process. We showed our product some fifty-odd potential customers. Each of the heads of sales loved the product, but every head of HR told that this had a clear potential for lawsuits (discrimination), and hence they wouldn't sign up.

We pushed for services sales, and our revenues started going up quickly. We reached an annual run rate of $3 million.

By this time my personal net worth had come to $150K!

Story of Ameri100

In a parallel universe, my brother Dev Nidhi received an e-mail from a friend to call him for an opportunity. Dev had had his own entrepreneurial successes and setbacks. So, when Dev called back his friend, he asked Dev to come to Philadelphia by the next Monday. Dev, who was in India, dropped everything he was doing and came to the United States.

This was in early 2013. A major chemical company had hived off one of its units to a PE-backed team. Dev's friend had become the CIO. He wanted some urgent help to fix one of the systems.

It started off as one project. Dev had to incorporate a company named Ameri & Partners Inc. literally in a day and start the work. By March of 2014, it had become too much work, and Dev wanted to build an organization around this opportunity. He asked why I was building one more services company—why not build it together?

I agreed, and Ameri acquired WinHire in May of 2014. I became the CEO of Ameri & Partners on July 4, 2014.

Three years and four months later, we became Nasdaq listed. In the next chapters, I will outline the strategies, plans, and actions that helped us get listed on Nasdaq.

As you read in the earlier pages, Dev and I had seen success and failure in equal amounts. Before Ameri, we had seen quite large setbacks. I had failed in a billion-dollar start-up! What that means is that you can start back up and still lead a company to Nasdaq in under four years.

We have structured chapters 3 through 9 in the following format. Although, please keep in mind that some chapters have Parts 2 and 3 clubbed together for the sake of simplicity.

> Part 1: Core concept—I explain the core concept and some basic information about this core concept.
>
> Part 2: How we applied it—I detail our steps in Ameri's journey using this core concept.
>
> Part 3: How to build your own—I give some other industry examples for you to adapt and make it your own.

Part 4: Further reading—I list books, blogs, and videos about this core concept for deeper understanding.

Here is a quick picture summary of the core concepts: I spent countless hours with Dr. Art Langer while I was doing my master's at Columbia University to arrive at a simple yet comprehensive framework to define what it takes to build a successful company. Dr. Langer guided me immensely in this exercise. Here is the framework.

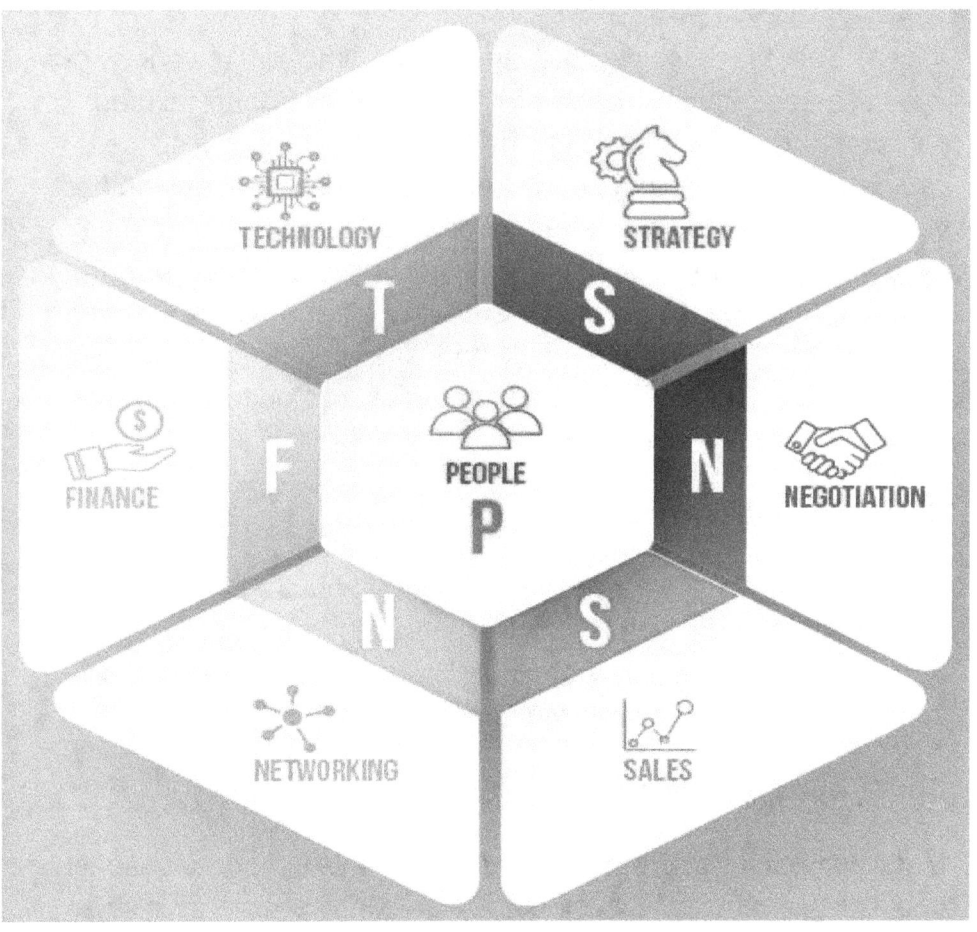

The acronym is "SN-SN-FT-P." This is all you need to learn to take your company to Nasdaq in four years or less.

I have also written a special chapter on vision, which is chapter 2 of this book. The chapters are summarized as follows.

Winner's Dream

This is the title of the book written by Bill McDermott. I will explain a few salient features of how to overcome adversity and still go on to become one of the best CEOs in the world.

Core Concept 1: Strategy

I have spent a considerable amount of time on a variety of business scenarios. In each of those successes and failures, I can simply trace it back to strategy. If the outcome was a success, you can trace it back to a good strategy. It doesn't matter whether you carefully crafted that strategy or you arrived at that strategy by taking mini steps. It boils down to that one thing: was the strategy, right? One thing is sure, in all my failures, as a postmortem, I have gone back and analyzed. I could always narrow it down to one or two bad strategies that led to severe bad results.

Core Concept 2: Negotiation

Everything in life is a negotiation. Whether you are in a business transaction or in a simple conversation with your family, every transaction leads to a negotiation. We will delve deep into the concept of better outcomes via formal negotiation.

Core Concept 3: Sales

Many companies and their CEOs miss the most important aspect of building a successful business: sales. Many people treat sales as a skill that they can hire or that can be outsourced. There is nothing falser than this. The truth is, sales cures all. In this chapter, we will dig deep into marketing, branding, and what it takes to build a successful sales team.

Core Concept 4: Networking

It's vital to understand that networking with the "right people" is a critical factor to take your company to Nasdaq. The most important aspect is to find the right people and relentlessly and subtly follow through to connect with the best people. It boils down to a simple formula: "give and take." In this chapter I will explain salient features of exceptional networking.

Core Concept 5: Finance

It's imperative for the founder or CEO to know all the fundamentals of finance. You may not know the exact financial entries or QuickBooks language, but you must know all the fundamentals of accounting, finance, and other Wall-Street language. This can be a book by itself, but I will explain in brief some of the most used terms and how to apply them to your business.

Core Concept 6: Technology

Even if your business is not a technology business, remember that technology is omnipresent. Whether you want it or not, you must know enough about the latest technologies. I will explain in detail the areas that will affect every business in the near future and how you can embrace the transformational aspects of technology to thrive in the ever-changing business world.

Core Concept 7: People

The statement that "it's all about people" is an old cliché. Yes, it is still all about people. You may have figured out all the SNSNFT part of the business, but if you have not mastered the art of people, then there is no way you can take your business to Nasdaq. In this chapter, I will walk you through how to hire a great team, fire nonperformers, and build a culture of excellence.

Nothing to Nasdaq

I will wrap up by summarizing all the aspects of taking a company from nothing to Nasdaq in under four years.

Chapter 2
Winner's Dream

Some accidental meetings change one's life forever. One such was meeting was with Bill McDermott, the CEO of SAP. This was in late 2014.

I had become CEO of Ameri on July 4, 2014 (easy to remember—American Independence Day!). My capabilities as a CEO were being internally questioned, as I am no expert in SAP, which was the highest revenue generator from one large client. This client was giving us 100 percent revenue to Ameri until I became CEO through the acquisition of WinHire. Then it was 75 percent or so.

I had told everyone that I was no expert in SAP; still, there were lingering doubts in people's minds. I was clear in my head with the SNSNFT-P framework of leadership.

At this time, we were still trying to figure out what should be the future road map for Ameri. I was evaluating multiple strategies.

I was attending a conference with a close friend of mine. We saw Bill McDermott in this conference. I told my friend that I would go and have a conversation with Bill.

Internally I was not sure at all. Here was Bill, who was super successful and a celebrity CEO running a $22 billion revenue and $120 billion market capitalization company, and me, Giri Devanur, a $8 million revenue company. The only common thing between us was that we are humans!

Even though I was reluctant, I mustered enough courage and walked up to Bill. I introduced myself and explained what we do. After a couple of minutes, Bill asked me, "In an ideal situation, if everything is aligned for you, what would be the biggest dream you would like to achieve?"

I did not even think, I guess, as I was still processing that I was talking to *the* Bill McDermott! I just blabbered, saying, "I would love for Ameri100 to be a Nasdaq-listed company," as this had been running in the back of my mind for a long time.

Bill immediately replied with his natural broad smile, "That, my friend, is a winner's dream. Go for it. It's an audacious goal to go after. This kind of goal is what will set a team up for massive victories. Since you are a SAP consulting company, I will be right behind you to support and cheer you!" And he told me what else must be done to get to Nasdaq.

I kept thinking, "That's a winner's dream." I was not sure what he meant by that. I was wonderstruck that he had spoken to me, a small company CEO. After a couple of months, I met Bill again in another event. By then he had already released his autobiography, *Winner's Dreams*.

I have met many CEOs around the world. I must say that Bill is one of the sincerest, an always positive and human leader who always inspires. I have heard this from all his colleagues. Even one ex-colleague who was fired because of low performance had great things to say about Bill. Think about that.

After our first meeting, my friend found a unique gift related to Bill's grandfather who played basketball. We bought that item, and we sent it to Bill. He really loved that memorabilia and immediately appreciated it.

After his book was released, I bought the book and read it a couple of times. The first time was kind of getting to know the background of Bill and his journey but when I read it the second time, I focused on the road for setting audacious goals and how to persevere with consistency, diligence and internal motivation.

In this chapter, I explore some of the ideas and thoughts Bill has discussed in the book *Winner's Dreams*.

Pinball

There is a small story that shows what makes a great company. It's the attention to small details. Bill had bought a deli as a kid, and he added pinball machines at his deli. This small addition increased sales and paid off the financing for his purchase within a year!

Winners learn that even a small addition can help you achieve impossible goals.

Quotations from Bill McDermott

1. "If you can connect dreams and details, you can achieve a lot."
2. "Optimism is a state of mind. It is built on the belief that you have the potential to achieve anything your mind conceives."
3. "I have no interest in mediocrity or maintaining the status quo, even if they're safer bets."
4. After losing his eye in an accident: "I am living proof that vision is not just what you see. My accident has given me so much strength, so much resolve, so much passion."
5. "First the vision, the strategy and the facts."
6. "Giving a customer credit—or even just respect—can make a big difference."
7. "Empathy to action is a race without a finish line."
8. "The prioritization of family in business cannot be stressed enough."

9. "What you focus on in life expands, and if you're going to focus on something, focus on the things that you're best at, and then do it better than anyone else in the world."
10. "Never waste time with small goals. They have to be aspirational. They have to be timeless. And they have to inspire people to go beyond the day-to-day business."

Giri Devanur with Bill
McDermott

Bill McDermott, CEO, SAP SE

Interview with Bill McDermott, CEO of SAP AG

1. **You had a spectacular journey from being a deli owner at sixteen to SAP CEO with a $140 billion valuation. Did you ever dream of becoming CEO of a global company during your teenage years?**

   I've always liked to work. Growing up, I had the opportunity to trade in three part-time jobs to become a teenage entrepreneur and run my own delicatessen business. I knew from a young age that I wanted to be somebody who would leave a mark on this beautiful world. If you're passionate about something, you have to want it more than anyone else. For me, it's always been about being in service to others—most importantly, to the customer. The customer and the customer alone is the boss.

2. **You are one of the most successful CEOs. How do you hire, train, and lead a team of extraordinary performers?**

   There's no room at SAP for small dreams. We want underdogs who never take anything for granted and who aren't afraid to exceed even their own expectations. We look for people who tackle every obstacle with their mind, their will, their heart, and their soul. Our employees—all eighty seven thousand women and men—are SAP's greatest assets. When you have a great team of people who care, a strong purpose, and a clear vision, you can achieve anything.

3. **How do you overcome phenomenal obstacles?**

I've always believed life's biggest challenges are our greatest opportunities. We're all going to get hit with our thunderbolt at some point. What's important to remember is to get up, get out, and get on it with. No one will ever remember how you fell, but they will never forget how you got back up and kept moving forward.

4. **You have seen hundreds of companies that show potential but don't make it to the finish line. What makes the DNA of breakout companies?**

First and foremost, you need to have a team you trust and believe in, because trust is the ultimate human currency. Companies also have to adjust to the next generation. Young people today need more than just the economics— they need a purpose-driven company that is committed to changing the world.

5. **What are the key aspects of becoming a great CEO? What is a typical day in the life of Bill McDermott?**

You can get anything you want in this life if you help enough other people get what they want—that's a lesson that has never gone out of style. Leaders have the unique opportunity to find the magic in a person. People will look to you for the permission to dream, for a clear path to help them rise and achieve that dream. You also have to build a culture that challenges people to build bridges rather than silos, to stay curious, and to always keep the promise. My days are filled with tackling interesting challenges and working with our incredible employees, customers, and partners all over the world.

6. **How important is it to have an overarching dream, or as you call it, a "winner's dream"?**

The unique thing about dreams is there's a perfect correlation between the size and scope of the dream and the outcome. Nothing can stop you from achieving your own winner's dream—be ever loyal to it and don't be afraid to dream big. Commit to your goals, write them down, and follow them with all your heart.

7. **What is your advice to a new start-up that would like to be listed on Nasdaq in a few years?**

Life happens between the lines—it doesn't happen through PowerPoints or corporate speeches. It happens when humanity consumes the moment. So, be human with each other, speak from heart, and, most importantly, be you. My mother, Kathleen McDermott, always told me, "Bill, just be you. The best part of you is you." I really believe that each and every person in this world should feel empowered to be exactly who they are. That's the privilege of a life well lived.

Chapter 3
Strategy Is *Everything*

Strategy is the most abused, misused, and misinterpreted word in the business lexicon. Many people mistake strategy as some complex scheme and tend to either overplay it or put over strategy into simple tactical items.

First, let's clarify what strategy is.

Part 1: Core Concept

The *Oxford English Dictionary* defines strategy as "a plan of action designed to achieve a long-term or overall aim." This definition is more from a political or military perspective, as originally strategy was the core of all warfare. In a pure business context, strategy is the process of defining an action plan and deploying resources to achieve a clear goal.

There are two major aspects of defining a strategy while you are preparing to take your company to Nasdaq under four years.

First: what you *must* do. This involves determining your goal, industry, core service offering, and so on. Here is a simple framework to develop your core strategy, which involves five W's and one H.

Why do you want to get on Nasdaq?

a._____

_____

b._____

_____

c._____

_____

What industry will you focus on? (Here you must be very clear about what core industry is fast growing, big market, and so on.)

_____

_____

Where are your primary customers? (Investors are becoming very particular about this aspect.)

_____

_____

When do you plan to list your company on Nasdaq? (Having a written date helps massively to prioritize your strategies.)

_____

_____

Who will be on your team who can help you develop strategies and action plans?

_____

_____

How do you plan to convert your strategies into measurable tasks?

_____

_____

Once you are done with what you must do, you and your team should work on the second part: what you will *not* do. Many theorists of strategy talk only about what you should do. But probably more important is to define very clearly what you will not do.

If you have read Steve Jobs' biography by Walter Issacson, you will recall one event that is supposed to have happened when he returned to Apple. At that time Apple had more than forty products and dozens of other products under various stages of development. Steve Jobs stopped a strategy session and walked up to the whiteboard. He wrote a four-quadrant matrix like the following:

	Desktop	Portable
Consumer		
Professional		

Steve literally ordered a stunned group of Apple engineers to kill all other products and focus on only four computers, two each for two groups of users.

"Deciding what not to do is as important as deciding what to do…That's true for companies, and it's true for products" (Steve Jobs).

Strategy is about what you *must* do and what you should *not* do.

Use the same questions defined above to come up with your own what *not* to do.

Peter Drucker, the great management guru who claimed "Culture eats strategy," was right for the industrial era. In the information era, if you don't have clear strategy, no amount of culture can help. Ask Nokia or BlackBerry. They had great culture but got the strategy wrong!

Chanakya's Three Questions versus Aristotle's First Principles

For a brief understanding of these two scholars, Aristotle was born 384 BC and Chanakya in 371 BC. For more on Chanakya, read https://en.wikipedia.org/wiki/Chanakya.

Both were in one way or another connected to King Alexander. Aristotle taught him and Chanakya strategized against him along with King Puru.

Aristotle taught on the basis of "first principles," as "the first basis from which a thing is known." More simply, he strongly believed in searching for the core or going to the basics of everything.

Chanakya taught three questions:

1. Kimartham karishyami,

2. Kim pratiphalam,

3. Aham saphalyam prapnomi?

The Sanskrit translation is as follows

1. Why am I doing it?

2. What might the results be?

3. Will I be successful?

If you can answer these three questions along with five W's and one H, you would have developed a clear strategy for your company to list on Nasdaq in four years.

Part 2: How We Developed Our Core Strategy for Ameri100

We were clear from the beginning that we would build a $100 million revenue company as fast as possible. By the time we had reached Nasdaq, we had grown Ameri100 from zero revenue to $50 million per year!

Here is how we evolved our strategies.

Why do you want to get on Nasdaq?

> a. We wanted to be on Nasdaq to get growth capital.

> b. Nasdaq listing would give us currency for acquisitions.

> c. We wanted to be the "only Nasdaq listed" SAP consulting company.

What industry will you focus on?

> The SAP consulting industry is large, with almost $200 billion in annual revenues spread over 180 countries. SAP also has become the world's largest cloud solutions provider with more than 130 million users. Ameri100 would focus on the SAP cloud, digital, and enterprise services market (what we called CDE).

Where are your primary customers?

> For the first five years, we decided to have all our customers in North America and delivery centers in India. As of today (January 2018), we have six sales offices in the United States and four delivery centers in India.

When do you plan to list your company on Nasdaq?

We had set July 2017 as the deadline (technically three years from the date that my CEO term began in 2014, but we got delayed by four months and got listed on November 17, 2017).

Who will be on your team who can help you develop strategies and action plans?

We had assembled brilliant employees, consultants, and advisors to accomplish our tasks. We had great lawyers, accountants, and financial modelers; our nonexecutive chairman who was a veteran fund manager on Wall Street; and so on. We also pooled some of our best resources in our company.

How do you plan to convert your strategies into measurable tasks?

We agreed in May of 2015 to make our Nasdaq journey into a two-phase approach. In Phase 1, we became an OTC-listed company through a reverse merger, and then in Phase 2 we chose the Nasdaq path by completing a one-year mandatory cooling period as expected by the SEC. It also helped us develop a discipline of being a listed company with annual reporting (10Ks) and quarterly reports (10Qs). During this period, we completed six acquisitions using the OTC currency.

Part 3: How You Can Build Your Strategic Model

After becoming the CEO of Ameri100 in July of 2014, I quickly worked on a project to define the core strategy. I had studied McKinsey's strategic model. Here is how we applied that theory.

McKinsey's Strategic Horizons

McKinsey's strategic horizons model forces you to spend all your energy on thinking about growth and how to innovate.

Ameri100 had a choice. Either we could have gone with one focus area, or we could have been a generic IT services firm. I came with almost zero knowledge of the SAP consulting market. I was more comfortable with financial services technology than SAP. I had to overcome my own biases and work on a different market strategy.

So, our team and I spent some considerable time and energy to define three horizons.

Horizon 1: Core Business

We clearly articulated that we were going to be a global leader in the SAP consulting market. I was very particular that we should have a simple acronym so that even our receptionist in India would be able to recite our core business in a simple statement. We called it ABCDE (Ameri's Business is Cloud, Digital, and Enterprise services in the SAP market). In this CDE offering, C and E were treated as core offerings.

Horizon 2: Emerging Opportunities

We initially thought we had figured out our digital transformation practice. We created a new team to work on digital transformation. This was supposed to take off immediately on a very large scale. Even though we did everything possible to make this work, unfortunately we were not successful in this strategy horizon. We rolled it back into our core offerings.

Horizon 3: Blue Sky

This horizon is all about taking business in new directions. We bought a company, and they had a product. Initial analysis showed that this solution was ready for a takeoff. We attempted a lot and eventually realized that the market was not ready. Even SAP faced challenges in that transition.

Strategy is about making choices, trade-offs; it's about deliberately choosing to be different.
—Michael Porter

Part 4: Further Reading

1. Avinash K. Dixit and Barry J. J. Nalebuff, *The Art of Strategy: A Game Theorist's Guide to Success in Business and Life.*
2. A. G. Lafley and Roger L. Martin, *Playing to Win: How Strategy Really Works.*
3. Michael E. Porter, *Competitive Strategy: Techniques for Analyzing Industries and Competitors.*
4. Robert S. Kaplan and David P. Norton, *Strategy Maps: Converting Intangible Assets into Tangible Outcomes.*
5. W Chan Kim and Renee Mauborgne, *Blue Ocean Strategy, Expanded Edition: How to Create Uncontested Market Space and Make the Competition Irrelevant.*
6. Sun Tzu, *The Art of War.*
7. Kautilya/Chanakya, *The Arthashastra Paperback.*

Chapter 4
Negotiation—Changing "No" to "Yes"

Here is an interesting story told by William Ury in his Ted Talk.

A rich man in the Middle East left his three sons seventeen camels when he died. His sons were surprised when they heard the division of camels he had left. The first son got one half, the second son got one third, and the third son got one ninth of the camels. The sons couldn't figure out how to divide the camels, as seventeen was not divisible by two or three or even nine. So how to divide the camels? The brothers got frustrated and went to the wise lady in the village. She thought for a while and said, "There is no easy answer. Add my one camel and see if you can solve your problem."

Suddenly they had eighteen camels. The first son got one half, which was nine. The second son got his one third, which was six. The youngest son got one ninth, which was two. If you add all of them, it adds to seventeen. They were still left with one camel. They returned the camel to the wise lady and headed out.

Problem solved!

That is the power of negotiation.

Part 1: Core Concept

The problem with most executives, entrepreneurs, and managers is that they perceive negotiations as a cunning, negative, and below-their-level activity.

Every transaction in life is a negotiation. Whether it is with a customer, a prospective employee, a buyer, or a seller, there is always a negotiation.

In day-to-day transactions of all sorts, you are bound to hear "no" as an answer to whatever you are asking for. If you have made up your mind to take your company to Nasdaq, you will hear many times "no" before you get to the victory line. Your board, your investors, your lawyers, the SEC, Nasdaq itself, and many other advisors may say "no" on your way.

You need to develop a mechanism to respond (not react) very carefully, understand why they are saying "no," and come up with valid answers to address their concerns so that you can shift their answer from "no" to "yes."

This is a subtle art, not the typical movie style as they show in *Glengarry Glen Ross*, the "always be closing" (ABC) mind-set. In your journey to Nasdaq, you will need to use a simple set of response mechanisms to get them to go from a "no" to a "yes."

Also, remember that negotiation is not a "win-lose" proposition. It is about making sure that you get what you want while others feel good too. A typical belief is that it must be a "win-win" negotiation. This is far from true. A negotiation can be a far more than "win-win."

Truly open-minded negotiators always look for expanding the outcomes to all parties involved. This is what they teach in professional programs like the one conducted by Harvard University's PON (Program on Negotiation). I highly recommend this program, as it has benefited me in multiple negotiations.

Here are the basics of negotiation.

BATNA—Best Alternative to a Negotiated Agreement

In negotiation theory, the best alternative to a negotiated agreement, or BATNA, is the most advantageous alternative course of action a party can take if negotiations fail and an agreement cannot be reached.

ZOPA—Zone of Possible Agreement

The ZOPA describes the intellectual zone in sales and negotiations between two parties where an agreement can be met that both parties can agree to. Within this zone, an agreement is possible. Outside the zone, no amount of negotiation will yield an agreement.

Hard Bargaining Top Ten Rules

The following rules are taken from the book *Beyond Winning: Negotiating to Create Value in Deals and Disputes*, by Robert Mnookin, Scott Peppet, and Andrew Tulumello (listed by PON).

1. Extreme demands followed up by small, slow concessions. Perhaps the most common of all hard-bargaining tactics, this one protects dealmakers from making concessions too quickly. However, it can keep parties from making a deal and unnecessarily drag out business negotiations. To head off this tactic, have a clear sense of your own goals, *best alternative to a negotiated agreement* (BATNA), and bottom line—and don't be rattled by an aggressive opponent.

2. Commitment tactics. Your opponent may say that his hands are tied or that he has only limited discretion to negotiate with you. Do what you can to find out if these commitment tactics are genuine. You may find that you

need to negotiate with someone who has greater authority to do business with you.

3. Take-it-or-leave-it negotiation strategy. Offers should rarely be nonnegotiable. To defuse this hard-bargaining tactic, try ignoring it and focus on the content of the offer instead, then make a counter-offer that meets both parties' needs.

4. Inviting unreciprocated offers. When you make an offer, you may find that your counterpart asks you to make a concession before making a counteroffer herself. Don't bid against yourself by reducing your demands; instead, indicate that you are waiting for a counteroffer.

5. Trying to make you flinch. Sometimes you may find that your opponent keeps making greater and greater demands, waiting for you to reach your breaking point and concede. Name the hard-bargaining tactic and clarify that you will only engage in a reciprocal exchange of offers.

6. Personal insults and feather ruffling. Personal attacks can feed on your insecurities and make you vulnerable. Take a break if you feel yourself getting flustered, and let the other party know that you won't tolerate insults and other cheap ploys.

7. Bluffing, puffing, and lying. Exaggerating and misrepresenting facts can throw you off guard. Be skeptical about claims that seem too good to be true and investigate them closely.

8. Threats and warnings. Want to know how to deal with threats? The first step is recognizing threats and oblique warnings as the hard-bargaining tactics they are. Ignoring a threat and naming a threat can be two effective strategies for defusing them.

9. Belittling your alternatives. The other party might try to make you cave in by belittling your BATNA. Don't let her shake your resolve.

10. Good cop, bad cop. When facing off with a two-negotiator team, you may find that one person is reasonable and the other is tough. Realize that they are working together and don't be taken in by such hard-bargaining tactics.

Part 2: How We Applied Negotiation in Ameri100

There were three stages of negotiations in Ameri100's journey to Nasdaq.

In the preliminary stage, our founder, Dev, negotiated a series of contracts with a new $5 billion company that was being formed. This led to building the foundation. It was a hard journey; as you recall, he started Ameri with nothing in hand. He had no office, infrastructure, people, or expertise. The only thing Dev had was a determination to make it happen.

Dev negotiated with dozens of specialist companies in the SAP ecosystem, agreeing that they would get paid once they delivered the project they were involved in. As you would expect, some of these projects took longer than anticipated. Some of the vendors couldn't be paid for months together. The only thing that kept the company going was honest and transparent communication with all parties involved.

After I became the CEO, we could start formalizing a lot of the relationships. We developed a formal vision and goal to get listed and raise capital on Nasdaq. We wanted to be the fastest company in the SAP world to get listed. We started pitching for investors. When we met with Lone Star Value Management, Jeff Eberwein, the CEO of Lone Star, was impressed with what we had accomplished. They were open to make an investment.

We signed a term sheet with Lone Star, and all the due diligence was completed. At this point we had news that one of our largest customers might wrap up their biggest project, and their revenue would significantly drop. We had a tough decision to make. We had to communicate bad news to our potential investor. These are the moments that define your journey.

One of my colleagues and I traveled to Connecticut and met Jeff and the team. We told them what had happened. We renegotiated the deal and gave them some discount to the deal that we had already negotiated earlier. We were very transparent and explained how we would recover from that situation. Our investor was happy that we had communicated and renegotiated the deal in a fair and transparent way. This was our BATNA.

Negotiation can be a respect-earning work!

In another situation, one of the employees who had agreed to join us and immediately go on to a project kept dragging his feet. We had been working on this key employee to take the assignment for a few weeks. Exactly on the day of joining, this employee tried to renegotiate his compensation upward in a very unfair way. We decided to walk away and explain to the customer. It was a tough call. We negotiated with the customer and agreed that it was better to have an alternative consultant. This negotiation was critical, as it sent a clear message to some of our partners that we would walk away from unfair negotiations.

We even negotiated with the SEC and Nasdaq. We had some situations where we had to work through our lawyers and negotiate with the SEC or Nasdaq. I was initially worried that the status difference between the SEC and a small company like ours would create a difficult negotiation. But as we progressed, I learned that it is all about having clarity and sincerity, and data will help in negotiation even with government.

Part 4: Further Reading

1. Deepak Malhotra, *Negotiation Genius: How to Overcome Obstacles and Achieve Brilliant Results at the Bargaining Table and Beyond.*
2. Roger Fisher, William Ury, and Bruce Patton, *Getting to Yes: Negotiating an Agreement without Giving In.*
3. Robert B. Cialdini, *Influence: The Psychology of Persuasion.*
4. Robert Mnookin, *Bargaining with the Devil: When to Negotiate, When to Fight.*
5. Stuart Diamond, *Getting More.*

Recommended training class: https://www.pon.harvard.edu/.

Chapter 5
Sales Cures All

Mark Cuban, the famous Dallas Mavericks owner, once said, "Sales cures all." There is no clearer truth than this.

Part 1: Core Concept

If you want your company to get listed on Nasdaq, unless you are some cancer-fighting drug research company like Tesaro, you must have a well-oiled sales machine. You may think, what about Facebook? If you search through their filings, you will notice even in their headcount, almost half of it is in sales and marketing.

Great sales and marketing helps you get the attention of the right customers, who in turn will give you the right contracts, which will help you attract better employees and investors.

Remember, the end of every job is selling. Whether you are a manager, a CEO, or an aspiring CXO, you must learn the fundamentals of selling. It's become fashionable to say, "I am not in sales." There is nothing further from the truth than that.

What Is Selling?

Selling is the process of convincing prospective customers that your product or service solves their problem or meets their requirement.

Customer Profiles

Columbia University professor Dr. Ran Kivetz told us in one class that there are only two kinds of selling: either you're selling Tylenol for headache (solution to a problem), or you're selling a cruise vacation (hedonic pleasure).

Be clear in your product or service classification. Is it Tylenol or a cruise? You cannot be both at the same time.

How Do You Sell—Direct or Channel?

You may choose to sell by having your own sales team or relying on a third-party sales channel. If you provide a product, then you can use online methods. I am not an expert on Business-To-Customer (B2C) sales; hence I will not dive deep into that aspect. If your business is a B2C model, please refer to other texts on that area. There are numerous resources available.

Sales Hiring

Building a great sales team is one of the biggest challenges for any management team. In some research, they have found that it costs $1.2 million for every wrong salesperson. This includes cost of hiring, salary for almost one year, replacement costs, training, and cost of missed opportunities in revenues and profit, and in some cases the cost of reputation, as a desperate salesperson may ruin the reputation of your company at a prospect forever.

The rule of thumb in sales hiring is if you hire three people, one will work out well, one will be average, and one you fire in six to nine months. It's a revolving door! There is no silver bullet for hiring great salespeople. It's a perpetual challenge for all companies. No CEO in the world will say we have cracked the code for hiring the best salespeople.

I remember reading a long time back about a manager in the United Kingdom who used to hire people who had the most expensive cars, apartments, and watches. His logic was, once people get used to luxury, they have no choice but to perform at that level, or else they will lose their luxury!

Hire the best sales team that money can get. This is the single most important area for the success of your company, and eventually this one area will predominantly decide if your company will go to Nasdaq.

Sales Tools and Processes

Make sure that your company has the right sales tools and processes from the very beginning. It is very important to map all your prospects, track their conversion, and always keep a healthy dialogue about why you are winning and what are the reasons you are losing.

It's critical to monitor why you are losing, as this may help you alter or completely pivot your product or service.

Also, having a formal sales tool, a customer relationship management (CRM) system, will force you to manage your budgets tightly under control. Whether you have one or twenty or one hundred salespeople, track everything like a hawk. If you are not that type of personality, then give the task to someone in your management team who has that focus and perseverance to track such data.

Sales Pitching

If you're pitching to a very important prospect, then you must spend a lot of time preparing your sales pitch.

There are multiple guides to explore this topic. Remember one key aspect: just visualize some of your vendors coming to pitch to you. How long will they be able to keep your attention if they have not come prepared?

Just keep thinking about your audience and prepare, prepare, prepare. It is said that even Steve Jobs used to prepare almost maniacally for his speeches. It is claimed that he once prepared one hundred times for a speech!

Part 2: How We Applied Sales in Ameri100

In Ameri100's journey to Nasdaq, we had some spectacular successes and failures in our sales.

Our founder did the first set of sales in a brilliantly different way. As I mentioned, we had none of the formal structure of an organization, given that he had started with nothing. But he assembled some specialists and won the first project.

Over the next twenty-four months, Ameri100 won some twenty projects by assembling almost one hundred partner firms from around the world. So, this was our virtual sales-and-delivery engine. In a massively critical engagement like the one we had, more than the slickness of the salesperson, it's about the content and delivery. That is why this model was so brilliant that we could assemble the best resources in the world and win assignments.

Initially we started off with some of the best consultants in the world, who had spent all their time for decades in working on multibillion-dollar companies. These consultants were super specialists in their areas of expertise. The customer could not have gotten these resources if they had given the contracts to larger companies, as these super specialists would not want to be lost in a large company.

In another case, we won based on a new business model. Here the selling was done on showing the customer faster, better, and cheaper in a completely different form from what the customer was used to seeing. We called it "outsourcing-3.0." In our view, in outsourcing-1.0, the customer would bring consultants in-house to execute some projects. In outsourcing-2.0, the customer would outsource the whole project to the consulting firm. The customer had no ownership of deliverables.

We offered a new model: outsourcing-3.0. In this model, the project is delivered one-third on-site and one-third off-site, and one-third is done using automated tools. The customer CIO was intrigued and wanted to try this new model. We successfully delivered a project by replacing a $10 billion global behemoth.

There was a third way we successfully executed.

We realized our industry was going through a vendor consolidation process. This normally means that a large multibillion-dollar customer cleans out their vendor list and prunes it to five to ten from, say, fifty to one hundred. This helps the customer in streamlining vendor management. They also put in a third party to manage the vendor resources, collect timesheets, pay them, and so on.

To overcome this challenge, we decided to adopt a new strategy. "Acquire clients inorganically and grow organically." With this strategy, we worked on an inorganic growth strategy. The basic idea is to identify acquisition targets that have rich customer lists but do not have a global delivery mechanism or partner network like what we had put together.

In the next twenty-four months, we acquired six companies, and our list of customers grew from five in 2014 to ninety-six as of December 2017! These were not small customers. These were multibillion-dollar-revenue customers spending hundreds of millions on their IT. We were doing just $2 million to $5 million in these customers. Our growth opportunities became infinite with those acquisitions.

It also expanded our sales team from two people to twenty. We started preparing all systems and processes for the coming years of growth.

We also kept trying to organically add salespeople. That has hit the same formula: one-third good, one-third average, and one-third fired!

Marketing

While sales cures all for sure, getting a formidable sales engine starts with marketing.

"Marketing is no longer about the stuff that you make but about the stories you tell" (Seth Godin).

We at Ameri100 were always pushing the marketing boundaries. Since we were very clear about our target market, we decided to have a powerful brand. The name Ameri100 was decided based on some very intense brainstorming. Initially we thought we wanted to be the symbol of freedom and completeness. Our objective was to serve America at that time, and hence we chose Ameri100. We drove our core values from our name:

Ambition   -   **Think big, scale faster**

Mastery   -   **We deliver perfection**

Excitement -   **It's in our DNA**

Reliability   -   **We do what we promise**

Integrity   -   **We always do right**

Then the question was about completeness. We added 100 to the end and called it 100 percent. There was a slight intelligent twist. If you see our logo, we added two zeros to give an impression that it was "1 to infinity."

Ameri100

Integrating brand, values, and positioning gave us a significant boost to our branding efforts.

Then later on while working on our S1 filing, one of the SEC attorneys asked us to define our services in simpler English. Obviously, we had made a complex statement to cover everything under the sun!

This observation by the SEC made me spend a quite a few sleepless nights. Then finally one early morning, it occurred to me that our offerings should be readable by a simple programmer to any investor. So, I named it ABCDE (Ameri100's Business is Cloud, Digital, and Enterprise services) CDE became our core offerings!

Even though many people want to believe that marketing has changed in the new digital world, nothing much has changed. It's just that the models of delivery have changed, and the attention span of people has dropped to less than four seconds (think of YouTube advertisements—even those four seconds we desperately want to skip). In this super competitive, hyper aggressive market, everything about marketing has to be about grabbing attention. But the core principles of marketing (popularly known as the 4 P's)— PRODUCT, PRICE, PLACE, and PROMOTION— still remain the same core.

We at Ameri100 were very clear from the beginning that for the first five years, the company would have these 4 P's as our core pillars of marketing.

1. PRODUCT: SAP—CDE (cloud, digital, and enterprise services)
2. PRICE: We were always one notch below Accenture and one step above offshore players
3. PLACE: We had decided our customers would be in North America and global delivery would be in India
4. PROMOTION: Given we didn't have the luxury of branding budgets, we took the guerilla marketing approach

Finally, you can have a great marketing machine, a fantastic sales team, a superb brand—none of that matters if you don't deliver to your customers accurately.

One of my mentors in my early days of Ivega taught me this simple formula: "Deliver to your customers—on time, within budget and expected quality." Nothing more…nothing less.

Part 4: Further Reading

1. Og Mandino, *The Greatest Salesman in the World*.
2. Dale Carnegie, *How to Win Friends and Influence People*.
3. Zig Ziglar, *Secrets of Closing the Sale*.
4. Neil Rackham, *Spin Selling*.
5. Tom Hopkins, *How to Master the Art of Selling*.
6. Brian Tracy, *The Psychology of Selling*.
7. Jay Conrad Levinson, *Guerrilla Marketing*.
8. Al Ries and Jack Trout, *Positioning: The Battle for Your Mind*.
9. Al Ries and Laura Ries, *The 22 Immutable Laws of Branding: How to Build a Product or Service into a World-Class Brand*.
10. David Ogilvy, *Ogilvy on Advertising*.

Chapter 6
Networking—the Art and Science

It's not about "what" you know. It's all about "who."

In your quest to build a company to list on Nasdaq, it's critical to understand the intricacies of connecting and building great relationships with the right people.

Part 1: Core Concept

One hundred fifty.

That's the number you must keep track of. It's known as Dunbar's number.

The theory of Dunbar's number posits that "150 is the number of individuals with whom any one person can maintain stable relationships."

What does that mean?

That means you can build and maintain meaningful relationships with 150 people. It's not the thousands of connections you have on Facebook, LinkedIn, or Twitter. If anyone claims more than approximately 150 relationships, they just don't know what they are talking about.

Even maintaining 150 meaningful relationships is a very hard task. This will involve your family, friends, classmates, and business associates. A meaningful relationship does not mean just sending some e-mail or a Christmas or New Year's card. It's about having meaningful conversations, helping each other, and so on.

In today's "digital avalanche" of content via multiple devices 24/7, it's difficult to have great relationships. It definitely needs consistent effort. Especially when you have set your sights very high on taking your company to Nasdaq.

Unfortunately, no formal programs will teach you how to network. It's trial-and-error all through the journey. Here are three stages of preparing for a great network.

1. Inventory: Go through your personal and professional network. Think how many people you really know. Now this has become really easy. Get a dump of all your cell phone numbers and go through whom you have called in the last year. If you have not called someone in the last twelve months, that person doesn't belong to your network.
2. Identify thirty members of your family and thirty of your personal friends (these may be your classmates, ex-colleagues, or your longtime friends). This is your private network.
3. Expand the list by adding thirty members from your own profession (rising stars, mentors, recruiters, salespeople, and so on). Identify another thirty people from other walks of life than your profession who are successful in their own fields. And keep some thirty for future contacts. All this adds up to Dunbar's 150!

Part 2: How We Applied Networking in Ameri100

As the foundation of Ameri100 was laid by our founder based on his networking skills, we wanted to cultivate that skill to the fullest extent possible. We had an initial challenge, which was overcome by building a coalition of small companies.

We identified all the requirements of our largest customer at that time. We had an opportunity to participate in more than two dozen projects. We built a list of some fifty companies that could offer expertise in those areas and reached out to each of them pitching for work. A lot of them responded positively, came into our network, and helped win and execute the projects. Some of our most senior consultants were independent subject-matter experts who had decades of SAP consulting expertise around the world.

Leveraging those skills was crucial for our successful launch of Ameri100. We rigorously continued that process of identifying and adding partners and built more than one hundred partners in a span of four years.

There were some interesting twists. I came into Ameri100 with no SAP skills. I was challenged by a senior consultant saying I did not have the right SAP connections. I took it as a challenge and reached out the global CEO of SAP, Mr. Bill McDermott. We got an opportunity to meet, and I developed a great relationship with Bill. He has since become one of my mentors!

We also took Dev's networking skills into our potential acquisitions list. During his half-million-mile flights, he met hundreds of SAP consulting companies. We kept evaluating these companies, and the ones we found interesting, we added to either our partner list or our potential acquisitions list.

We completed six acquisitions based on such networking and have more than twenty-one companies for future acquisitions in our pipeline. This way we kept our strategic acquisitions pipeline in a healthy mode.

Another area was my network with one of my investment-banking friends. He has been my friend, partner, and mentor for more than eighteen years. When we wanted to raise capital, he introduced us to the right investor, helped us through the capital-raising process, and helped us complete the transaction in record time. This move also helped us become OTC listed, as our chairman, who is a Wall Street veteran, advised us that reverse merging into an OTC-listed company would give us currency and help us build the discipline to become a Nasdaq-listed company in eighteen to twenty-four months. This move helped us immensely to become Nasdaq listed in four years!

It's Give and Take

A lot of people think networking is about asking someone you don't know. Unfortunately, the world doesn't work that way. You must give first something that makes the recipient happy or thankful. Only then can you anticipate something in return.

Also, networking is not for the people who don't commit time, effort, and, in some cases, money.

Here are some tips:

1. Networking is about building long-term relationships.
2. Build an area of expertise and share your passion in that area.
3. Smile and be positive—no one wants a negative person in their network.
4. Do enough homework/research about whom you want to network.
5. When you meet them, listen to them carefully.
6. Learn body-language dos and don'ts.
7. Be respectful of time, culture, and political opinions.
8. Remember to follow up.

Part 4: Further Reading

1. Keith Ferrazzi, *Never Eat Alone*.
2. Leil Lowndes, *How to Talk to Anyone: 92 Little Tricks for Big Success in Relationships*.
3. Daniel Wendler, *Improve Your Social Skills*.

4. Jeanne Martinet, *The Art of Mingling: Fun and Proven Techniques for Mastering Any Room.*

5. Olivia Fox Cabane, *The Charisma Myth: How Anyone Can Master the Art and Science of Personal Magnetism.*

6. Patrick King, *Bulletproof Confidence: The Art of Not Caring What People Think and Living Fearlessly.*

7. Aston Sanderson, *Small Talk: How to Talk to People, Improve Your Charisma, Social Skills, Conversation Starters & Lessen Social Anxiety*

Chapter 7
Finance—Cash Is King

Thirty percent of all start-ups fail because they don't manage their cash properly.

As you prepare your company to go on Nasdaq, make sure you have enough cash in hand. There is a simple formula here. You can raise only one-third of the money you want in two times the time you thought needed.

What does this formula mean? It means that if you need $6 million in six months, be prepared to get $2 million, and that takes twelve months minimum! This is the hardest lesson I have learned as an entrepreneur/CEO running multiple start-ups.

A long time back, when I was working on building a system, my then boss, now mentor, asked me if I knew anything about balance sheets. As a programmer then, I didn't have a clue about that. I honestly told him that I didn't have a clue. He gave me a lot of hard time and told me that if I wanted to progress, I needed to learn how to read financial statements.

I took that lesson from him and ordered some one hundred company balance sheets. Remember, in the late 1990s and early 2000s, companies still used to send balance-sheet copies. Over the next twenty-four months, I read almost one thousand balance sheets.

The first few dozen balance sheets didn't make any sense at all. It was like picking up an Italian novel and trying to read when you have no clue of the language. After thirty-plus documents, I started seeing some trends. Being a programmer, I was able to physically do some "pattern recognition" and started to get comfortable. Here are some highlights.

If you are a well-qualified CPA or MBA in finance, you can skip a few of these basics and jump to the next chapter.

Part 1: Core Concept

There are three primary areas of finance any senior executive must understand: accounting, corporate finance, and pitching.

Accounting

1. Income statement
2. Cash-flow statement
3. Balance sheet

There are millions of books and online resources about these. You can easily find enough resources even on YouTube as well. As my intention is not to fill this book with fundamentals, I will leave it to you to figure it out.

If you are a nonfinance executive who is aspiring to be in the leading positions of a company that aspires to go to Nasdaq, I would highly recommend taking a few weeks of finance class. Almost all prominent colleges run "finance for nonfinance professionals," and there are classes on Udemy or Coursera.

Once you learn how to read these three fundamental sections of a financial statement, you must read at least a few dozen financial statements of some of the companies you know. Start with companies in your industry, as you will know the fundamentals.

A company is naked in a 10K.

Unless there is some crazy management team that is willing to go to jail, companies disclose everything in the United States.

There is a specific reason why companies disclose everything and more in their 10Ks (annual reports) and 10Qs (quarterly reports). There are some five thousand companies that are listed on Nasdaq and NYSE, put together. For this small universe, the United States has almost eighty thousand securities lawyers! That means for every listed company, there are more than ten lawyers outside waiting every minute to see if a company makes a small mistake. They pounce on such companies, take them to the dry cleaners, and suck the money out. This should not come as any surprise knowing some of the craziest fines and settlements in the US history of litigations.

Over the years, the United States has become extremely regulated. In 1996, the United States had over 8,000 companies, and by June of 2016, the number had reduced to 4,333! This is probably because of overregulation and the fear psychosis created by a litigious culture that has spread like a cancer. No experienced CEO or CFO would want to certify everything that is happening in the company as though they have control over every little detail! And the CEO and CFO will have to personally guarantee that there is nothing unknown or hidden deep inside the company, or else they risk everything to be hounded by the wolves.

Despite all these obstacles, if you have a genuine business and no intention of hiring and taking an investor for a ride, the pubic markets are very supportive. Nasdaq primarily gives you three major things:

1. Access to capital (both debt and equity become much easier)
2. Currency (for acquisitions as well as hiring great people)
3. Global branding

Corporate Finance

Once you learn how to read these three accounting sections, you must move into corporate finance.

Despite all the buzzwords such as IRR, NPV, P/E, and so on, you need to understand that there are again three core areas of corporate finance.

1. Planning and budgeting
2. Allocation of resources
3. Financial control

Let's discuss each of them.

Planning and Budgeting

Any investor would want to see your business plan. He or she wants to know how you are planning to generate revenues, what your expenses are, how you have made assumptions, and so on. I am sure investors would have seen hundreds of business plans, and their BS detector will be very high. So, make sure that your team has spent enough time on the planning and budgeting process. If you don't have an expert, get an expert to help you.

Allocation of Resources

Once you have enough capital, the investors will want to know how you are going to deploy that capital. How much of that will come in as revenue, how much will be equity, what will happen to the gross margins if the sales increase or decrease, and so on. This will also help you decide whom to hire, when to hire, what type of infrastructure you need, and so on.

Financial Control

It's imperative for any company aspiring to be listed on Nasdaq to have adequate financial controls in place. Remember—there are too many hungry securities lawyers looking at everything you do. Make sure that there is proper structure and that everything is audited by a qualified CPA and signed off. Having a highly integrated finance system like SAP is recommended. Remember, within forty-five days from closing a quarter, you must file a 10Q. That means you must recognize all your revenues and expenses, come up with all financial statements, and have a management discussion section in the 10Q. Trust me; it's a lot of hard work.

Once you understand what goes into a 10Q and a 10K, your appreciation for your finance team will shoot up immensely.

Pitching

One of the most neglected areas of finance is pitching. Unfortunately, they don't teach "how to pitch" in any finance program. At Columbia University, I took it upon myself to start a class on pitching!

You may have the best business plan, a very good deck and team ready, but if you have not learned the art of pitching, then all your hard work will be a waste.

When you are ready to meet an investor to raise any level of capital, be it seed, venture, private equity, or public equity, you must have mastered the pitching of your story.

You must practice numerous times. I have done hundreds of pitches in my life, and in the latest round we did forty-three pitches in fifteen days. What I have learned from this continuous pitching is that the only thing that matters is to practice, practice, practice.

There are again numerous articles and videos on YouTube about how to pitch. I have a deck that will explain the fundamentals of pitching on the NothingToNasdaq.com website. Please download and read it.

For a successful capital raise on Nasdaq or otherwise, make sure that you and your team are fully prepared. I cannot stress this aspect of preparation enough. The more you are prepared, the better. There is nothing about being spontaneous or extempore. Every word, every sentence must be rehearsed many times.

In our journey to Nasdaq, I have led more than one hundred pitches to all types of investors such as angels, VCs, PE, hedge funds, retail, and mutual funds. Every time, there was a new lesson or a twist. There was nothing like a perfect pitch. Remember, the other side players are experts at cutting any froth that's in your presentation.

Also, make sure that all your numbers are tied properly. What I mean is your income statement, cash-flow statement, and balance sheet in your financial model must be properly connected, and the flow through should be accurate. You cannot have any errors anywhere.

Your pitch document is also scrutinized for the validity of your assumptions. How will your revenue and profits impact IRR for the investor? Will a drop in revenue severely impact your EPS (earnings per share)? Will your SG&A changes significantly impact the cash flows?

These questions need a full year or two years' worth of preparation to answer accurately. You need to do all these things while running and building successful sales, marketing, operations, and other aspects of business.

Nobody ever says it's easy to get listed on Nasdaq.

Part 2: How We Applied Finance in Ameri100

We had an added complexity in our finance function. All of our finance team except our CFO was in India. Imagine running a core function like finance literally on the other side of the earth and with a twelve-hour time difference.

What could have been a very frustrating experience, we put enough effort into making a process-driven organization. We ensured that all our accounting and finance functions worked some overlapping hours with the US offices and got the continuity of operations.

We put together a team of experts in corporate finance as consultants. We hired a whiz kid in Mumbai to help us build the business model. He laid such a fantastic groundwork for our financial model that one of the investment banks whom we used in our Nasdaq journey told me that out financial model was one of the best that he had seen in a very long time.

We also trained our internal team along with consultants to prepare for the SEC reporting and so on. These consultants were truly world-class and came up with one of the finest prospectuses I have read. And I have seen many companies of our size.

Initially when we went through the reverse merger and became an OTC-listed company in 2015, our investor and chairman and his team really helped us walk through the nitty-gritty of becoming a listed company. I would give very high marks to that team for having patience to train me and our finance team to become fully conversant and efficient in timely filing of 10Qs and 10Ks.

Our legal counsel used to joke that our team would file 10Qs and 10Ks at the real last minute. I have had some really hard times holding my breath at 4:59 p.m. when our document was getting uploaded to the SEC website. Once, we had uploaded 90 percent of the 10Q, and there was a technical glitch. The SEC site refused to accept it, as it was past five o'clock. We had to present the SEC with the screenshots of the technical issue we faced in uploading, and then finally the SEC reluctantly accepted that we had technical issues!

We are probably the only US company that has its full finance team in India as well as probably the only company that prepared its investment prospectus fully from India.

With numerous late-night calls and countless hours of overtime working, our finance team in India mastered the art of closing books both quarterly and annually in the required time. I would put this as one of the highest accomplishments of our finance team.

Part 3: How to Build Your Finance Team

Hiring a Great Finance Team

As you build your finance team, you will realize there are two core capabilities that are a must. One is the bean counting, aka accounting. This is primarily to keep the books balanced and clean. As you plan to become a listed company, this team should be able to close the books of accounts in forty-five days or under. This is very hard and harder than most of us who are nonfinance professionals think. Even though there are systems like SAP itself, it is very hard close the books of accounts in an accurate and timely manner. This is an inward-looking function.

The second part of the skillsets you will need is to have a corporate finance team. This means, can your team produce a great financial model, deal with lawyers and outside financial institutions, and so on? This is about raising capital for the growth of the company. This is a more outward function.

Unfortunately, you will almost never find a CFO who can do both. I have tried many times to find a team that can do both. It is almost impossible.

OTC Listing—Pros and Cons

We took an unusual route for a Nasdaq-bound company. We were looking initially to raise private equity money and grow before we got to a certain size and got listed. But when we met our first institutional investor, he advised that being on OTC is like learning to swim in a four-foot pool versus a wild river like Nasdaq. This was appealing, as I did not have any experience of listed-company management. I had raised earlier angel, VC, private equity, and so on. But never public capital.

Though there were many pros, there were cons as well with being an OTC company. The liquidity and trading volume were very low. So, the stock would move wildly up or down with few hundred shares being bought or sold. Also, since we were aggressively pursuing an acquisition-led growth strategy, this was a big hurdle.

Whiz Kids

I realized it would be futile to try and hire a CFO who could do both internal and external roles. I asked the present CFO to step down and started actively looking for someone who could fix our internal issues rather than outward issues.

Then, I wanted to bring in a financial-planning genius to our team. I tried all my known contacts and couldn't pull the right resource. Hence, I published a requirement on Up Work, a freelance consultants' website. After four or five days, I had a flurry of résumés wanting that work. Finally, I chose one guy who referred his friend instead of himself.

We established a great relationship soon. This guy was a whiz kid. He developed a business model, which was so good that one of merchant bankers told me that they will use that financial model as a template for all deals going forward!

So, you do get lucky in hiring whiz kids!

SEC Reviews and Forty-Nine Comments

We filed our first version of an S1 prospectus with the SEC in mid-April 2017. We were advised by a banker that we should get an approval very quickly in a few weeks. How naïve I was to believe that. After four weeks we got our first comment letter with twenty-three comments. We took four to five weeks before we filed the responses. After that the SEC sent another fifteen comments. It took another six weeks to respond for us. I was hoping it would be over. Then the SEC surprised us again with ten more comments. Finally, they had one verbal comment. So, we went through some agonizing five months of waiting and doing pretty much nothing during this period. Our lawyers had clearly instructed us that we could not engage in any acquisition-related activities during that period or any activity that could affect the ownership structure of the company.

Changing Bankers

We had some extra drama that was happening. We had selected one banker to help lead us to Nasdaq. After we filed with the SEC, we realized that we had to change the banker. We lined up a banker and let the earlier banker know that we were terminating the contract. After that termination, we realized that the banker who had committed to us was backing out.

There were some very anxious moments, and we retained one more billion-dollar bank. The MD of this bank and I traveled to India as part of their due diligence, as we have all our back office in India. We established a great personal relationship.

After all the due diligence, this bank also stepped back, citing some silly reason. Luckily for us, we had signed two bankers this time, and the other bank was kind enough to take the whole mandate and run the show.

This was truly like changing the tires of a car when you are driving at ninety miles an hour!

Part 4: Further Reading

1. H. George Shoffner, Susan Shelly, and Robert A. Cooke, *The McGraw-Hill 36-Hour Course: Finance for Non-Financial Managers 3/E* (McGraw-Hill 36-Hour Courses).
2. John A. Tracy and Tage Tracy, *How to Read a Financial Report: Wringing Vital Signs out of the Numbers*.
3. Wayne Label, *Accounting for Non-Accountants, 3E: The Fast and Easy Way to Learn the Basics*, Quick Start Your Business.
4. Stephen A. Ross, Randolph W. Westerfield, and Bradford D. Jordan, *Fundamentals of Corporate Finance*, 11th ed.
5. S. M. Rambhia, *Stock Market Investing for Beginners: Fundamental Analysis: Learn Fundamental Analysis Basics for Stocks Investing*, Investing Books for Beginners.
6. Steven M. Bragg, *The CFO Guidebook: Second Edition*.
7. Martin Soorjoo, *Here's the Pitch: How to Pitch Your Business to Anyone, Get Funded, and Win Clients*.
8. Oren Klaff, *Pitch Anything: An Innovative Method for Presenting, Persuading, and Winning the Deal*.

Chapter 8
Technology—Software Will Eat the World

This is the easiest and yet most complex piece of the puzzle, which is very hard to understand and put together in the journey to Nasdaq. To say technology has been changing fast in the last twenty years is truly an understatement. Technology has been changing superfast every year for the last fifty years.

Intel cofounder Gordon Moore in 1965 noticed that the number of transistors per square inch on integrated circuits had doubled every year since their invention. The simplified version of Moore's law states that processor speeds, or overall processing power for computers, will double every two years.

And we haven't stopped since then. In 1993, Marc Andreessen wrote his Mosaic browser to connect easily to the Internet. The next year he renamed the product Netscape, and world has never been the same since the IPO of Netscape in 1995.

What Netscape did was to make it really easy for personal computers to connect to the Internet. Before that you had to have been a geek or a student to connect to the so-called Internet. I remember using 9600 bits per second baud rate modems to connect to computers in the United States. And it used to take forever to dial in. Getting connected to a server or another computer seemed like winning a jackpot!

So much has progressed since the mid-'90s. Today we get restless if it takes more than ten seconds to connect to a website! Thanks to pioneers of the Internet in the mid-1990s and early 2000s, we have moved faster than any other time in human history in terms of technological advances.

Now we have 3.8 billion users worldwide as of June 2017. Remember, in December of 1995, there were just 16 million users. Growth of 237 times in twenty-one years! It is simply incredible to see so many people around the world connecting to Internet.

Whether you are a technology business or any other business, new technologies will disrupt your business every three to five years. As Marc Andreessen put it clearly in August 2016, "software will eat the world."

Part 1: Core Concept

There are two ways your business will get disrupted if you are not agile and super active in identifying the changes that are sweeping across all businesses.

First, your own products or services will get disrupted by a new player or a smarter competitor who is risking it all. This will be done by a faster, better, and cheaper product or service. If you are not continuously upgrading, changing, and moving at extremely high speeds, your company will become a dinosaur. Think of BlackBerry and Nokia in recent years, who had 95 percent of the control over the mobile-phone industry till early 2008. In just nine years they have been reduced to less than 2 percent and faced bankruptcy. In May of 2016, the Nokia CEO ended his speech saying this: "We didn't do anything wrong, but somehow, we lost." He literally cried! You should watch the YouTube video.

No one in their wildest dreams could have predicted in early 2008 that Apple and Google would be the most dominant mobile players ever!

Think again— "We didn't do anything wrong, but somehow, we lost." In today's business world, it is not about "not doing wrong."

It's about being at the forefront of the change. And that change is dominated by technology, especially software.

The second part of the problem is that the industry you are serving and your customers get disrupted. It's almost like saying that you were the number-one supplier of keyboards of smartphones to BlackBerry and Nokia. They are really big customers, cash rich, and pay you well. Your order book is great, and everything is sailing so smooth. And this visionary called Steve Jobs introduces a phone with no keyboard!!

Could you have done incremental innovations? Could you have put some engineers to make your keyboards little better? I am sure you get the point.

The smarter thing is to be paranoid. The other legendary leader of Intel, Andy Grove, famously said, "Only the paranoid survives."

Are you paranoid enough?

To solve these challenges, a company that is going to Nasdaq must constantly look at their own business, their customers' business, and disruptors. This must be reviewed monthly. In the good old days, pre-2000, you could examine these aspects once every two to three years and have a five-year business model and so on. Reviews used to be annual. In today's disruptive world, if you don't look at it on a monthly basis, your survival itself will be at question.

This is not about just tech products. Imagine you are a distributor of diapers, and you did not foresee Amazon buying Diapers.com and disrupting that entire industry.

Or you are a taxi operator. You think you're coasting smoothly, and then comes Uber.

There are too many examples from the last twenty years and even ten years that will show that five-year business models are dead. But unfortunately, the SEC, Nasdaq, and a whole host of investors still think one can predict five years ahead and expect you to have a five-year business plan based on today's business environment.

There are no simple answers. As technology is a great enabler, it can hurt as well.

For your company, look to technology as an enabler to do everything in all of the SNSNFTP framework (Strategy, Negotiation, Sales, Networking, Finance, Technology, and People). For ease of use, I am outlining the basics and tools to use.

1. Strategy—Use technology to define and maintain a strategy map. For example, use a framework like the 7S model of McKinsey and draw a strategy map using freely available or paid software. It does not matter which tool you use, but build a discipline of reviewing the strategy map on a monthly basis.

2. Negotiation—Keep track of all elements of negotiations the company has done in the past and track every aspect of the negotiation, even as basic as an Excel worksheet. Whenever you have to enter a new negotiation, go back to the list and see what worked or not. This knowledge will save you millions of dollars.

3. Sales—It is more than obvious to use a CRM system and a bunch of other tools related to marketing. It's no longer a technology fantasy. Technology plays at so many levels in sales today. Would you think airlines? Watch "United breaks guitars" on YouTube.

4. Networking—Use LinkedIn and Google Plus, and if you want more specific research on a customer or investor, there are really sophisticated technology tools such as Ranking.

5. Finance—If you don't have a well-oiled finance team with the best software, forget getting on Nasdaq. Remember, you must file quarterly and annual reports within forty-five days of closing the quarter! You cannot do it without the help of the best technologies.

6. Technology—Use technology itself to monitor, visualize, and strategize the impact of technology on your business and your customer's industries!

7. People—Not only must you use technology to source, hire, train, lead, and measure people, but you also should look for people who are open to adapting to the ever-changing world of business, which is getting eaten by software. People are everything, which we will discuss in the next chapter. But if they are not tech savvy, your company won't progress to Nasdaq.

Part 2: How We Applied Technology in Ameri100

Ameri100 services technology to its customers. Since we were the new kids on the block and we did not have any serious amounts of capital and resources, we truly started off as a "company in the cloud."

1. Partner network
2. People network
3. Infrastructure in the cloud
4. Virtual offices

5. OT-IB-EQ

Partner Network

Ameri100 started with nothing in hand. No technology, no infrastructure. Our founder put together an agile network of partners and executed the first client's projects. Over time, we built a network of world-class super specialists in each area of our clients' requirements. As of today, we have over one hundred partners around the world in various specialties in our service offerings. This helped us scale immensely fast. Collectively our partners had more than forty-five hundred people. This allowed us to compete against the big players in the industry.

People Network

We have always believed in the "just-in-time" model of resourcing. This is clearly against the industry practice in which players on average keep about 30 percent of the headcount on the "bench." This helps them shift around resources as they win new projects. In our case we did not have the luxury of keeping resources on the bench. We had identified probably about fifty individual expert consultants in various specialty areas. We had to maintain almost a real-time tracking of the consultants to help us in our projects. I am very thankful to some of our senior consultants who went beyond the requirements and helped us in winning our clients' business.

Infrastructure in the Cloud

We literally started off with everything on the cloud. Initially both in Ameri and WinHire, we set up our e-mail on Google, and we did work on our clients' projects on the cloud. We also connected to all our vendors on the cloud. What I have realized in the past three years is that new-age companies will not have any technology infrastructure. It will be some combination of

Google/Amazon/Microsoft systems that will help you build. Once you scale up, then you will migrate to something more robust like SAP.

Virtual Offices

Between the end of 2013 to almost mid-2015, we operated with zero office space. All we had was a "registered office" in Delaware, and the rest was all a combination of Starbucks, Marriott lobbies, and hotel rooms, as well as our consultants' homes. As virtual workspace is zooming with We-Work type players, going forward I don't see companies having physical offices. It will be interesting to see how Nasdaq and the SEC will view a company that operates everything in remote or virtual offices. Whether it meets listing standards will be a good legal question!

OT-WB-EQ

As one of my mentors passed away last year, I fondly recalled his coaching for me. I was in my late twenties, and we were walking in Geneva. He had told me there is a simple three-step formula for building a successful business.

> OT: On-time delivery. Customers love when you deliver on time or just little ahead of time. We have made this our founding principle.

> WB: Within budget. Customers hate you if you run over on your quoted budget. No one likes such surprises.

> EQ: Expected quality. There is nothing worse than for a customer to get something that is of inferior quality. We put all our efforts into delivering the exact quality that we promised. This helped us repeatedly win businesses.

This magic formula of OT-WB-EQ is true whether you are running an e-commerce business or a restaurant chain. As you build business to list on Nasdaq, think of everything from a customer-service aspect and use technology as a primary lever.

Technology is no longer just an enabler as in the past. It has become the core of everything you do.

Interview with Nandan Nilekani, Chairman of Infosys

1. You (Infosys) were the first Indian company to get on Nasdaq. What made you to list on Nasdaq?

We were the pioneer company to go on Nasdaq. It was a major leap forward. It required deep understanding of US Accounting, SEC filing, how to go to Quarterly reporting, how to present your results, transparency, how to engage with analysts and talk about business. It was a multiyear journey. It was very important because the clients of Infosys were global clients, for them the fact that Infosys was a US listed company, practicing US Accounting and transparency, having US investors was a great source of solidity and reassurance. It had a direct benefit on perspective of business more so from the point of branding.

2. What preparation was necessary to list on Nasdaq, that too being a pioneer?

Infosys was incorporated in 1981, listed on the Indian exchange in 1993 and listed on Nasdaq in 1999. We were the pioneers in this and It was a journey of 18 years. It was important that internal systems are geared for that. Good predictability of the system, Quarterly reporting, ability to automate internal accounting technologies were all equally important. This results in major leap to bring focus on what you need to do to reach here. Setting standards for Corporate Governance, Technology and Business. Infosys was the first to create a company of professionals under the leadership of Narayan Murthy, first to share ownership with employees, believed in middle class values, believed in high standard of Corporate Governance and demonstrated transparency. All these factors enabled us to list in Nasdaq.

3. You are considered as the person who lead the world's largest and complex technology project UiDAI. How do you see global enterprise businesses get affected by complexity of technology?

Being the founding chairman of Aadhar and UAID gave me great experience in managing the world's largest project. It was also working in the Government setting. It was also about designing for scale, designing for sustainable architecture. Simplicity of design was very important because we realized that simplicity is the heart of sustainability and It was built completely using Open Source Stack. That was the first experience with Open Source in a big way. We took a decision in 2009 to use Open Source Stack long before it was accepted (Using Hadoop, MySQL, Linux, Apache). Open Source has tremendous capability and can build any enterprise. Today after coming back to Infosys, the learnings from both Aadhar and as well as my experience working with startup as well as the experience building an education learning infrastructure to transform learning taught me a great deal about how technology is built in today's world. How it is agile devops automated real time, whole new culture of quick build systems, rapid evolutions. Great to bring those learnings back to Infosys. Working on these projects have taught me how technology is built in today's world of rapid evolution, agile and automated real time. On time within budget with expected quality. That was the mantra. Aadhar was built within budget before time with great product quality in a government set up. Today there is an expectation that the product should do plus. Expected to be innovative and transformational. We have to come up with solutions and ideas because the customer wants the best with strength, robustness, reliability and management with innovations in the new world to manage the disruptions. With the pace of innovations, disruptions have only gone up. Big implications and new challenges for new incoming players in healthcare, insurance. Continuous innovation to help the transformation and add value. Company that brings both these to the table is going to win this game.

4. Nandan has attributed "World is flat because of technology" and now Marc Andreessen says " Software eats the world", Where do you this will lead in future?

We are now at a point of technological inflection where many things will be done with not only software but a combination of Software+ Algorithm+ Data. That is going to become pervasive. Our job is to how to use that to amplify the business of our company. How can our business be grown and delivered with a better customer experience using all these things? That's what the game is all about. When we combine software + algorithm + data, the other thing that happens is it allows the automated system to learn about an area they don't know anything about. If your business model is dependent on some knowledge base. The knowledge base itself can be eroded by these technologies. So, it's a very transformational point in nature of business and data is a big part of that. So, it's a big opportunity for our customers to leverage all these things

Lot of work I do in education is about enlightening the future of learning. It's not all about getting a degree and then working for 30 years based on that knowledge. It is about continuous learning. It is about anytime anywhere learning. It is about just in time learning. We are not going to have one job in our career but multiple jobs with multiple skills are required. Some jobs that we have done will become obsolete or will be automated, new jobs will be created. The only way we can flourish in that is by being able to learn how to learn and using that to quickly learn new things, So the education system has to be geared to that world and lot of work we do in education, not at Infosys is oriented towards this way of thinking about learning. A massive reorientation required on education.

5. What is your advice to a new startup to think of listing on

Nasdaq in a few years?

What you need is a great team. I have spoken to lots of investors, venture capitalists, entrepreneurs, finally what matters is the quality of the people we have. Everything else falls into place. We can figure out strategy, pivot your strategy, pivot your business model but we cannot pivot the quality of the people. They are the heart of it. So, we need a great team, who has a united purpose. The reason why Infosys was successful was there was unity of purpose, they were all in the same page, doing the same thing. They believed in long term, believed in deferred gratification. The journey of 12 years from inception to IPO in India. It took Infosys 18 years to be listed in Nasdaq. This required persistence stamina, willing to postpone your rewards, requires ability to deal with adversity and bounce back. So, having a great team of people is the most important thing, everything else will fall in place.

Part 4: Further Reading

1. Clayton M. Christensen, *The Innovator's Dilemma: When New Technologies Cause Great Firms to Fail (Management of Innovation and Change)*.
2. Andrew Grove, *Only the Paranoid Survive: How to Identify and Exploit the Crisis*.
3. Louis Gerstner Jr., *Who Says Elephants Can't Dance? Leading a Great Enterprise through Dramatic Change*.
4. Walter Isaacson, *Steve Jobs*.
5. Tony Hsieh, *Delivering Happiness: A Path to Profits, Passion, and Purpose*.
6. Kevin Kelly, *The Inevitable: Understanding the 12 Technological Forces That Will Shape Our Future*.
7. Alec Ross, *The Industries of the Future*.
8. Ben Horowitz, *The Hard Thing about Hard Things: Building a Business When There Are No Easy Answers*.

Chapter 9
People—One versus Thirty

The following statement is attributed to Steve Jobs from 1995:

"The difference between a company with superb programmers vs. average ones is 30:1."

And some say it was 25. Some even claim that he said 100:1.

One thing that is sure is that the difference between great and average is phenomenally high. It is astonishingly clear that it's always better to have that superb person on your side than an army of averages.

Part 1: Core Concept - Volition

For a long time, as a CEO in my earlier ventures, I believed that we can take average people and make them extraordinary. That was so faulty in logic.

I used to believe that people can be motivated. Unfortunately, motivation is like sugar or cocaine. It gives you a high for some time and eventually fades out. And the aftereffects are terrible. Just like any other addiction, you need that substance more and more, and if you stop feeding the beast, it comes back as withdrawal syndrome.

What you need to do is to hire people who have volition. The dictionary meaning of volition is "a choice or decision made by the will."

You need to hire people who do not need any kind of external motivation. And based on my experience of being a CEO for the last two decades, this is one area that makes or breaks a company.

Manage?

I have a simpler formula. I tweeted this a while back one fine morning when I was dealing with an HR crisis: "If you have to manage someone, you have hired the wrong person."

Think about it. If you have a person who must be told what to do, how, when, where, and so on, then you have hired the wrong person. If you hire the right person, you will not have to tell him or her what should be done.

This is extraordinarily important.

Step 1—Hire Right

The cost of a wrong salesperson is $1.2 million in the United States. I am sure that in most parts of the world, the cost is equally astronomical.

While we were working on WinHire, my product start-up, I realized that hiring salespeople was one of the hardest problems every single company faces. I stepped on so many research notes on why we make such crazy hiring mistakes. I have made millions of dollars of hiring mistakes.

Research tells us that "we make hiring decisions in approximately 14 seconds from the moment a candidate comes into your office. We scan the person from top to bottom, a handshake, an eye contact first few words/sentence, and bingo your subconscious mind has made a decision. Then next 30 minutes to an hour, your conscious mind validates the decision already made by asking leading questions as well as interpreting even the answers to validate the already made decision."

This mental bias comes from the fact that, as humans, we like to work with people who are like us, dress like us, smell like us, talk like us, and so on. This is why there is hardly any diversity in most parts of the working world. So how do you overcome these built-in human biases and still hire great people?

Here is a list of steps you may consider while building your "superstars" team:

1. Make sure that you do need to hire a new person. Ask whether outsourcing or automation can take care of this position, or whether one of your current employees can handle this as an additional role.
2. Wait for a few days to see if you really need to fill this position.
3. Build a detailed a job description for the position. (This helps in defining the skills part of the person.)
4. Then build a personality description (look for the attitude and behavioral aspects of the person).
5. Decide to pay above market salary. Never hire a cheaper-than-market resource.
6. Again, look internally to see if the company has anyone who can fill this position or if you can automate. You don't need to motivate software.
7. Define a clear, watertight interview process. Make sure that at least four rounds are done. Some must be in person, and make sure one or two of them are over phone or video to make sure that normal human biases do not play their roles.
8. Make sure that any one of the interviewers can reject a candidate. Hiring should be based on full consensus.
9. Never hire the first candidate available. You should build a short list of at least seven resumes and go through their interview process before you finalize an offer.

10. Never hire when in doubt. The cost of a wrong hire is crazily high.

Never, ever hire someone based on your gut factor. That will eventually turn out to be a gut-wrenching act. Stay away from such hiring.

Hiring is an art and a science. Make sure you give equal weight to both factors.

Step 2—Retain Your Best

It's probably easier to hire great people than retain them. Why? Because when they are so good, the market will know, and your rivals and competition want to poach your talent.

There is a war for great people. Remember, the value of a great resource is equal to thirty times that of an average person. Many companies and CEOs have figured this statistic out. If you want to lead a company to Nasdaq in four years, you must learn every trick in the game to hire *and* retain your best talent.

Here are the top ten things you must do to keep your best talent.

1. Make sure that you have the compensation right, as best you can, all the time. People care about their compensation a lot. There are vague theories that say it does not matter. They are wrong!
2. Make sure that your best resources in the company get the highest compensation. Remember, people do talk about salaries. They will compare even if you do not want them to. And once they find that an average person is getting an equal or higher pay, they will immediately start looking out, and you will lose your best person in no time.
3. If you think your top resource is looking out, probably they are. Start talking to them immediately. Address whatever

concern they may have about the company, future prospects, growth opportunity, and their career plan. Sometimes, all that your top resource wants is to be heard. So, listen carefully. Don't be judgmental.

4. Give people ownership. This is about making them part of the family. A Nasdaq-bound company must make sure that all key people see that vision and get a complete sense of ownership. Issue stock directly or through stock options.

5. Invest in top performers. Send them to additional trainings. Send them to learn a new skill or master one that they already have. Hire experts to train your best people. Investing in your own people is the best way to show gratitude.

6. Keep them challenged. Great resources always want the next big challenge. They always thrive in such challenging environments.

7. Reward them regularly. Make sure that your HR team recognizes the efforts of top performers and always rewards them. It is not about just some annual gala awards function. People truly appreciate sincere appreciation. Even a pat on the back and saying "great job" by a CEO can go a long way. Be sincere in appreciation. If you can add a small gift along with the appreciation, that will take it a long way.

8. Your best people expect strong loyalty. Loyalty is a two-way street. You can't expect loyalty if you don't give it.

9. Be there during their tough times. If they are going through a personal challenge, be there. If they have a health issue, be courteous. People remember all these gestures, and they will return the favor ten times.

10. Finally, never criticize them in public. That is one thing top performers hate. All brutal criticism can happen in a closed-door meeting but never in public. Make it a habit to praise in public!

Step 3—Hire Slowly and Fire Fast

We tend to drag what's supposed to be a commonsense and straightforward formula. I have been accused by my colleagues as a guy who gives a long rope to nonperformers. I have tried to address this problem many times. I have not been very successful in assessing people for what they are worth and firing people who don't deliver.

As I stated earlier, my philosophy has been that "if you have to manage, then you have hired wrong person." This belief has led me to not fire people fast enough. Lately, I have started doing monthly assessments of my colleagues at a much deeper level than any other time, and hence I was able to see the facades people used to hide their nonperformance.

As you lead your company to a successful Nasdaq listing, you must put systems and processes to evaluate people on a monthly basis. This is critical for the longevity and sustained success of the company.

Here are some tips on firing:

1. Think through it before you fire anyone. Does this person need some training to improve, or is he or she going through some personal challenges that need support, and will he or she perform better?
2. Never humiliate anyone while firing. Firing itself is very stressful for the recipient. Think if you're on the other side, how would you react?
3. Never fire an employee on the phone. Period.
4. Always give a couple of weeks' warning before firing. This saves a lot of trauma for the employee. They may simply quit before getting fired.
5. Always have a witness while firing. This saves a lot of legal challenges in the future.

6. Keep the meeting as short and polite as possible.
7. Have a clearly defined transition plan.
8. Listen carefully when the employee is talking.
9. Avoid compassionate statements. They simply don't work. It makes you look like a phony character even though you may be genuine.
10. Finally, do firing graciously.

Part 2: How We Applied People in Ameri100

Ameri100 started its business in a rare situation with no capital, no teams, and no infrastructure. It had to evolve its own set of methods to travel from nothing to Nasdaq.

There are three phases of role playing by different sets of people in our journey.

In phase one, when Ameri100 was executing its projects with its only client, the projects were coming in as though it was a fire hose. Our founder and a couple of initial consultants were running all over the world to get the execution partners. It was an abundance problem after a few months. Too many projects to execute.

At the end of phase one, I remember we made an offer to one consultant who was instrumental in the early successes of Ameri100. That offer was to become the CEO of Ameri100 with 15 percent equity. This consultant, whom I respect very much professionally, accepted the offer in the morning only to come back in the evening to reject it. I have been amazed at this decision even till today.

Then we attempted to bring in a "professional CEO," a more nonentrepreneurial manager to run the company. We interviewed a bunch of candidates and finally zeroed in on one of them. This candidate had a fine résumé and good credentials. But after a month we realized that he was totally not the person we were looking for. His priorities proved to be on the wrong side of what we had anticipated.

So, we exited this person very politely and moved on to the next stage.

In the second phase of Ameri100, on July 4, 2014, I was made the CEO. I was presented with a very difficult situation. Our founder and the original team believed that the first client was still going to give a $120 million business. I was skeptical. I kept challenging them. I clearly remember in one meeting I told the team that "there is an elephant in the room. This client may decide to go, and we have very little course correction left." And unfortunately, four to five months after my becoming CEO, that client completed the major initiative, and the revenue that was flowing into Ameri completely stopped.

Handling this crisis, which I had anticipated, I had visited our potential investor. Just two days before closing the deal, I went to our investor's office and declared that we might lose this top client, and I offered a discount to the deal we had negotiated. Our investor appreciated the honest presentation of data and transparency we displayed. And they accepted our 10 percent discount offer and invested in Ameri100. This was a great lesson for me personally. Transparency is the best policy with all classes of people, be it an employee, customer, or investor. Keep telling the truth. With that financial closing, we also became OTC listed on May 26, 2015. Thus, we prepared our company for the next stage of growth.

In the third stage, we continued our growth story and completed six more acquisitions. Each acquisition was a big challenge in terms of people. Every company, however small or big, will have their own culture. This cultural aspect of every group of people becomes a vital challenge when a merger integration happens. And we had six of them in a short span of eighteen to twenty-four months. Imagine all the chaos in terms of culture and integration. This phase was filled with political battles, turf wars, and games people played. As a CEO, for me, it was one of the biggest challenges. How do you satisfy the egos of all founders? I had sixteen people directly reporting to me. I kept managing everyone's expectations, and till the end of 2016, I managed all sixteen of them. At the dawn of 2017, I cleaned up my org chart and reduced the number of my direct reports to six. It was a massive effort in order to bring more order to the chaotic organization. It was a humbling experience for me managing all these founders.

Interview with Rudy Karsan, CEO of Kenexa IBM Inc.

1. **You built a great company, Kenexa, from scratch. What was your motivation to start?**

   I've been one of the luckiest guys. I wanted to start Kenexa primarily because of three kinds of greed—first, obviously money, second was the thrill of unknown experiences, and third was the greed for learning. I am not a PhD or anything like that. I was born in Kenya and at every stage of my life, I kept experimenting with various things in life. I wanted to start a company which will help customers to find "right person for right job". It was a simple mission, and we got lucky again and again.

2. **Do you believe in hiring the best people or hiring average and making them great?**

   I have always known my strengths and weaknesses. I never thought I am some superman and could take an average person and make them great in the work environment. That doesn't mean that all people are not great. They may be better than me at playing an instrument or sports or some other area. But, in my philosophy, you bring in the best people to the job and allow them to thrive in the given opportunity. On a lighter note, hiring is like arranged marriage versus love marriage. There is never a clear answer to say which is better. It depends on many other aspects of life.

3. **What are the best practices you used in hiring great people?**

I look at hiring from three compartments. First aspect is, if the candidate is hardworking, how smart and how much passion he or she brings to the job. Second aspect is what are the internal drivers like ego, greed, and fear. And third aspect is of behavioral like luck, grit, and resilience.

4. How did you handle it when you had to fire some of your best people?

I've always thought there is no good way of firing people. I have gone through a lot of agony when I had to fire some people. As I always segmented all our colleagues into three baskets. One was my partners. They are like an extended family. It's not about just financial relationship; it is about emotional and mental relationship. Then I had second group of people who were strategic employees, and these were really critical resources. Both hiring and firing these were extremely challenging decisions. Third group was regular colleagues. I always made sure that when we had to let go some of these people, my partners and strategic employees handled that. I just made sure that the exit was honorable and equitable by paying a decent severance and so on. Bottom line is, there are no simple ways of firing people.

5. What are the best practices a company must adopt to retain great people?

I keep going back to my three segments of partners, strategic employees, and other colleagues. You should make enormous efforts to make sure that first two groups are paid at or above markets and make them part of your life. Be transparent with them. It is all about handling people with respect. If you treat people well, you don't need to do any extra effort to retain your best people.

6. How long did it take you to lead your company to Nasdaq?

Kenexa was originally founded in 1987. Kenexa went through three distinct periods. First was of initial baby steps. Then we decided to bring in an investor. After than within four years, we were listed on Nasdaq. We chose to grow very aggressively, and then finally IBM made an offer, which was a very decent offer. After that Kenexa is going through a global growth story.

7. What made you sell your Nasdaq-listed company to IBM?

Life is all about timing. As I mentioned, I have been very lucky. What happened was suddenly post 2010, there had been a lot of activities in the human capital management space. First, Oracle bought Taleo talent management solution for $1.9 billion. Then SAP went out bought Success Factors for $3.4 billion. Both Taleo and Success Factors were our direct competitors. So suddenly we were competing big boys of IT business. So, there was a combination of fear and rational reasoning that we must be a part of a larger company led us to merge our business with IBM.

8. What would you do differently if you had to lead a start-up to Nasdaq?

Not really. I have always enjoyed what I did. And I have never spent too much time worrying or crying about my decisions. So, if I had to lead a start-up again, it will be the same way. Enjoy the ride, have fun while you're serving your ultimate boss—the customer!

Part 4: Further Reading

1. Daniel H. Pink, *Drive: The Surprising Truth about What Motivates Us.*
2. Geoff Smart and Randy Street, *Who.*
3. Simon Sinek, *Start with Why: How Great Leaders Inspire Everyone to Take Action.*
4. Geoff Colvin, *Talent Is Overrated: What Really Separates World-Class Performers from Everybody Else.*
5. Daniel Coyle, *The Talent Code: Greatness Isn't Born. It's Grown. Here's How.*
6. Malcolm Gladwell, *Outliers: The Story of Success.*
7. Angela Duckworth, *Grit: The Power of Passion and Perseverance.*
8. Anders Ericsson and Robert Pool, *Peak: Secrets from the New Science of Expertise.*
9. Matthew Syed, *Bounce: Mozart, Federer, Picasso, Beckham, and the Science of Success.*
10. Jim Harter and Marcus Buckingham, *First, Break All the Rules: What the World's Greatest Managers Do Differently.*

Chapter 10
Nothing to Nasdaq

Chapters 3 through 9 clearly established the skills framework (SN-SN-FT-P) that is necessary to get a company to Nasdaq.

Now let us look at some of the fuzzy areas that are also critical to lead from nothing to Nasdaq. There are ten most important aspects of leading through this roller-coaster ride.

1. Drive

There is nothing more important in attitude than drive. You must drink endless amounts of Kool-Aid to be able to ride this journey of nothing to Nasdaq. Even though it looks so easy to lead a company through the ups and downs, you must have ton of drive. This cannot be built overnight. It's like a muscle in your hands or legs. You must consistently work at it.

Success is never guaranteed in any pursuit. Even companies that were built with a lot of capital and talent can go out of business. This type of experience can be disheartening, and many people could be inclined to give up on their goals in the wake of failure.

There will be days when you simply want to give up and move on in life. It's those days when you need your internal drive, which should take over and get it going. After failure, even though celebrated in the Silicon Valley perspective, summoning the drive to keep going, an indomitable will, is necessary.

2. Focus

To make your business venture super successful, you have to become crystal clear on the focus of your life. It is about both business and your life. Focus comes not just from picking what areas you want to work on; it's also about which areas you refuse to work on. Honestly, the number should be almost one to ninety-nine. That means you should know which ninety-nine things you don't want to work on and the one thing you must focus all your energies on. That kind of focus will help you build great success.

3. Persistence

There will be naysayers, and your own closest friends and family will not believe that you will succeed. It is the human mind in them, which expects you to be like them. Water always finds its lowest level. Only when you apply persistent pressure does water go up, right?

In the same way, almost all your friends will tell you how hard it is to succeed, how disastrous it will be for you mentally, physically, financially, emotionally, and so on. They will all be thinking that you are mad.

I have had my share of these. I had one of my closest friends say to my face that I will never be able to build a $50 million business. I had one advisor and one other closest person question my sanity to think that I can lead a company to Nasdaq. This happened three or four weeks before our Nasdaq listing!

In such circumstances, you must persist. Nothing can help you but your persistence.

4. Curiosity

In building a great company, you will face so many challenges. A very important quality you must possess is intellectual curiosity. The clichéd term everyone uses is "out-of-the-box thinking."

As you face new challenges literally every day, you should keep a calm mind and look for newer solutions. If you do not have a curious mind to come up with newer solutions, make sure that in your team, there are people with such characteristics. And listen to their ideas for new solutions.

5. Dissatisfaction

One of the hallmarks of great companies is that they are never satisfied with what they have. The moment any company becomes satisfied with their product or service, that is the beginning of the end. Being unsatisfied is critical. Remember what happened to Nokia, BlackBerry, and so many other companies who dominated their markets and became satisfied with their product or service. And those companies face extinction faster than anything else.

6. Patience

This is a contrarian attitude for a leader who wants to lead the company to Nasdaq in under four years. I struggled with this one all the time. At times, I used to be so frustrated with some of my colleagues who refused to move at my speed in executing some work. I used to be tempted to jump in and take care of the task at hand. Some of my advisors warned me about my own burnout if I jumped into all tasks. So, grudgingly, I had to develop this trait, which is very unnatural. Even though internally you are impatient for the overall vision, you must develop the patience on tasks and allow people to perform one at a time.

7. Optimism

To be optimistic when you are internally feeling that you are sinking is the hardest part of life. Your team doesn't want to know that you are also doubtful of the outcome of something important you are all working on. This is when hiding your emotion and training your brain to be optimistic is hard. The chemical serotonin in the brain helps the optimism triggers. This chemical gets generated by carbs. So, if you are feeling a little low on optimism, go treat yourself to a good doughnut!

8. Unrealistic Goals

Normal authors write how you must be realistic about goal setting. If you want to set fifteen years to take your company to Nasdaq, then you can go with that approach. But here we are discussing how to get to Nasdaq in four years or under. This is not going to happen if you set "realistic" goals. You need to be massively unrealistic in setting goals for yourself and your team. I remember having heated debate with our team and board members about our Nasdaq listing. Even our lawyers had expressed concern that we were moving too fast, and there was a clear possibility of failures. Being unrealistic in goal setting and perseverance helps in such situations.

9. Thick Skin

There will be a lot of skepticism, negative vibes, questioning the sanity of the leader, and laughing behind your back in your journey to Nasdaq. Some people will tell it to your face that you are a fool to dream of taking a company public on Nasdaq. The numbers are overwhelmingly in their favor. In 2016, there were approximately six hundred thousand new business start-ups. But the number of IPOs was just 105. With such alarmingly low rates, a Nasdaq listing is a distant dream. Even business owners and entrepreneurs don't expect to take a company public; forget just working folks. That is why you need thick skin to ignore all negative feedback and push forward on your dream.

No one can climb Mount Everest with thin skin.

10. Luck

Finally, does luck work? If anyone tells you that luck didn't favor them, they are lying.

Luck plays a massive role. You may accept or not. It is really luck that will help you cross the finish line.

What is the classic definition of luck?

Success or failure apparently brought by chance rather than through one's own actions.

There are hundreds of things that can go wrong. And trust me…they will go wrong. With all those things that can go wrong, you must navigate through this massively complex journey to list on Nasdaq.

You will realize that it is not just hard work, team, and all the other aspects I have described in this book.

Bill Gross, one of the most respected VCs in Silicon Valley and the founder of Idealab, in his TED2015 talk, asks the audience to guess which factor is most important to start-up success. And he goes on to explain what drives success. He identifies idea, team, business model, funding, and timing as the common factors. He studied hundreds of companies and concluded that most successful companies got the timing right.

In my view, it is just plain and simple luck.

Existence of God

I know a bunch of rationalists, and my twenty-year-old self would not have believed that God exists.

I strongly think that my brother, Dev, who founded Ameri, and I, who founded WinHire and other ventures, earlier wouldn't have agreed that God's hand helped.

1. What is the probability of Dev getting a call from a CIO friend asking him to travel overnight to the United States to kick-start a company?
2. There was no way Dev could have figured out the delivery of such a complex project without the first two consultants that came onboard and worked for six months for free. Is that just coincidental?
3. After I became CEO, I would have blundered one key decision. That day, one older gentleman who had come to our office accidentally started talking about some other company and how they made an error that resulted eventually in closing down the business. This triggered me to stop making that error and saved a lot of money and potential troubles. Is that an act of God, or is it something else?
4. And finally, on the day of Nasdaq listing, at 9:23 a.m. there was a technical hitch. We assembled a call with bankers, multiple lawyers, advisors, and our own team. While everyone was scrambling for an answer about how to fix this error, we did not have an answer till 9:29 a.m. At 9:30 a.m., the trading had to start, and we had no clue of what would happen if the trading didn't start that minute. At that moment, someone in Nasdaq took a call and solved that glitch, and the trading started at exactly 9:30 a.m.

AMRI100 is listed
on NASDAQ

Giri Devanur at the listing of
AMERI100 under NASDAQ

God, the universal power, or sheer coincidence (for nonbelievers) shows up and helps you in such situations. You must be ready with 99 percent of the effort. The last 1 percent is some unknown intervention. That is being *lucky*.

www.ingramcontent.com/pod-product-compliance
Lightning Source LLC
Chambersburg PA
CBHW071215220526
45468CB00002B/619